INTERPRENEUR

The Secrets Of My Journey To Becoming An Internet Millionaire

By Simon Coulson

'I never lose. I either win or learn.'

Nelson Mandela

ISBN: 9781910602997

First published in 2016 by How2Become Ltd.

CONTENTS

ACKNOWLEDGEMENTS

Thanks to Mum - for making me, shaping me and supporting me.

Nan Marsh (RIP) who was always able to rustle up a great meal and a 'survival kit' whenever I called in at the end of a long day's work in the City, and who was an absolute inspiration for her work ethic.

For Harley Coulson - always making me smile. Aged 7, he already dances better than me and tells better jokes.

Rachel Murphy for her expert assistance in putting this book together.

Everyone I worked with at BT - especially Barry Smith, Geoff Richardson, Sean Gubbins, Chris Wingate, Colin McNulty and Clive Bayley.

Gary Gee and In The Red for hiring me for my first band.

Everyone in all the other bands I've played in, including (though I expect I've missed some) The Cold Tuesdays, Jonus, Shiandra, Ouija, High and Dry, Melle Butler, Julia Jones and Glen Kirkham (I think you still owe me for that studio, Glen!)

Dan Slowly, Steve Jenner and Rick McMunn for 10+ years of memorable, fun times on the road with Coolplay.

Steve Foley for starting my speaking career, Andrew Reynolds for giving me a shot at the big time and Ernesto Verdugo for making me an international speaker. (As I write this I've just been asked if I am potentially available to speak at the ExCel in 2017, at the same event as Barack Obama. This would not have happened without you guys - watch this space!)

For the great office team that helped build my businesses especially; Debbie, Charlotte, Sophie, Nigel, Nick, Alannah and Becca.

For the current *Internet Business School* team; Ben Brophy, Stas Prokofiev, Gino Cirelli, Jason Gee, Jay Hastings, Julia Haydon and

Claire Perry, and all those who have helped along the way.

For the fantastic team that made the Darling Buds dream come true; Peter Foord, David Cox, Cosmo Lindsay, Damian Mactavish, Andrew Chapman, Roger Norris and Nici Norris, Courtney Delieu and Lucy Ridgwell.

Martin Sutton for the latest chapter with The Songwriting Academy and all of our amazing mentors and students.

Finally, as a thank you to YOU I'd like to give you all a free course on Internet marketing, covering essentials like hosting websites, automation software, website building, SEO, software tools and much more.

Go to *Interpreneur.com*/resources to find out more and to find links to the resources mentioned in this book. You will also be able to register for updates to the book and find great training tips.

PROLOGUE

'You alright mate?'

I looked at the stranger in a suit standing over me and tried to work out where I was and what had just happened.

My back hurt and I was lying at the bottom of a busy escalator. Other people were pushing past and stepping over me, some of them tut-tutting and catching me with their bags and heels.

I frowned and my head throbbed as I muttered a reply to the concerned man looking down at me.

'Yes, I think I'm alright . . .'

I'm not sure whether my words came out as clearly as that because my brain felt fogged, but that is what I tried to say.

'Someone's gone to get help for you, mate. Hang on.'

Other strangers arrived. They were in London Underground uniforms and one was wearing a fluorescent jacket with the word 'paramedic' written on it. The staff lifted me into a wheelchair and the medic began to take my blood pressure and ask if I was diabetic or suffered from any other medical conditions.

'No,' I stammered. The fog was lifting and I was beginning to feel embarrassed. 'There's, er, nothing wrong with me . . . I think I just blacked out.'

'I see. Can you remember what happened, before you fainted?'

In hindsight, that was a very big question. What *did* happen before I fainted?

The very last thing I remembered was stepping onto the escalator at King's Cross tube station and then there I was at the bottom, dazed and confused and asking myself *how did I end up here?* The reality was that I'd collapsed from exhaustion on my way home from work. My body had simply had enough, which is hardly surprising, because an awful lot of other stuff had happened before I fainted that day.

For 14 years, ever since I left school, I'd been climbing up the corporate ladder in customer relations at British Telecom. I'd done this very 'successfully' as I had been promoted time and time again, although I say this with scepticism now as I've learned that this statement depends on how you define success. Despite the regular increases in pay, perks and my position in the company, slowly but surely I'd become trapped in the rat race. I was commuting for two hours each way on top of working extremely long hours, often six or seven days a week. What's more, I was so institutionalised by work I hadn't even realised how bad things were, and how unfulfilling my life had become.

What is life about? I asked myself after I'd dusted down my suit and my pride that day and got myself to the mainline station. Crammed in a busy carriage, squashed up next to other grey-faced commuters and surrounded by the smell of take-away food and stale sweat, I thought back over the years and wondered how I'd let myself be sucked into this existence. I was 32 years old. Surely there had to be more to life than this? Surely I didn't have to do this for the rest of my working days?

My collapse had given me a sharp wake-up call. It was time for change, but what was I going to do? How was I going to shake up my life and make my dreams come true?

CHAPTER 1

The Wake-Up Call

What am I doing here and what is life about? They were the thoughts suddenly going through my mind after my collapse at King's Cross. I'd worked for British Telecom PLC for 14 years after my parents had persuaded me to do my A levels and get a job with a large company. 'It's a job for life,' they told me. 'That's what you want, Simon. Stability. Security. That's what you get from a large corporation.'

Dad had worked as an accountant all his life. He had built up a small, steady local business that just about kept the roof over our heads and food on the table. It wasn't exciting or glamorous, and in fact it seemed pretty boring to me whenever Dad talked about his job. I never questioned Dad's choice of career though, or the amount of money he earned. Being a small accountant inevitably meant that Dad's clients were often start-ups that quickly went out of business, leaving him unpaid. Unfortunately his business never progressed beyond the bottom end of the food chain in terms of size. The strains and pressures of the continued bad debts he was lumbered with and the long hours he worked meant that Mum and Dad decided to split when I was around 11.

Shortly after this my mum, brother and I moved to a small end of terrace in an unremarkable street in Gravesend, Kent (think Coronation Street). We didn't have cash to spend on luxuries, but we certainly never went without. That was something to be proud of, but of course Mum wanted my elder brother and me to do better than she and my dad had. That is why she encouraged both of us to work for a big company, one that would provide the corporate cushioning my father never had as a small town, self-employed accountant.

My brother chose to work for British Telecom and was doing well, and so when it was my turn to leave school – St George's in Gravesend, which later fell into OFSTED special measures - I followed him into the company, becoming a BT trainee working on customer relations systems. It seemed like a sensible choice at the time and my parents were delighted I'd heeded their advice. So there I was, on the corporate hamster wheel, getting up at the crack of dawn to put on a suit and commute into London from Kent every day.

In the early years it was fun – a lot of fun, actually. Suddenly I wasn't a boy and I was becoming a man. At 18 I was working mostly with colleagues in their 20s and 30s which was great as I could learn from them. I enjoyed the challenges of my job; I worked hard, kept my head down and got my reward with an annual pay rise of around 5%. So far, so good.

I also learnt some really valuable lessons from my early managers about different styles of management. These lessons have stuck with me to this day. For instance, Barry Smith, a straight-talking Yorkshireman, was one of my early line managers. I have never forgotten Barry. If I asked him a question he would often just reply 'RTFM' (read the 'f******' manual) then turn his back and carry on with whatever he was doing. He did this even when he knew the answer, which was very frustrating to a young lad like me who wanted all the answers, fast.

At the time I thought Barry was just arrogant, because why wouldn't he just tell me the answer? How irritating was that? However, I realise now (at least I'd like to think this!) that what Barry was teaching me was that I should go and find the answers to my own questions and not rely on others to provide solutions. In hindsight Barry's style of management made me develop a 'can do' attitude and this has stood me in very good stead on my journey from BT to Interpreneur. The ability to 'RTFM' probably got me some of my subsequent promotions at BT, and as my story unfolds you will learn that 'RTFM' was a very important lesson indeed as I flew the BT nest and discovered the wonderful world of the Internet.

Barry also taught me how to take what I would describe as a 'bare bones' brief for a project and action it. His thinking was that what's crucial is to get to the destination and fulfil the brief, but the way you get there isn't so important. In other words, Barry didn't mind HOW I did something, so long as I ultimately delivered what was required. This worked to my advantage, because it made me think for myself instead of just following step-by-step instructions or a tried and tested formula.

I remember one specification for a task literally being written on the back of a 'fag packet' – Benson & Hedges, to be precise! Such a seemingly cavalier start to the project didn't matter because it was successfully completed in the end, and along the way I was learning all the time, picking up tips and ideas and testing out strategies as I went. The way Barry encouraged me to work was as creative as it could get in the essentially rather dry and boring corporate job I was doing. The freedom I had to plough my own field was refreshing and illuminating, although it wasn't like that for very long.

Unfortunately, BT soon implemented no end of quality control initiatives such as 'Total Quality Management', which meant my 'fag packet' days had to come to an end. Red tape and no end of rules, policies and structures to adhere to put a stop to the 'bare bones' brief philosophy I was used to working by. The bare bones were replaced with incredibly detailed briefs that were often extremely stringent and rigid, and of course I had no choice but to toe the line.

Nevertheless, I was young and keen to do well and I threw myself into the job year after year. One Saturday I went in to the office on overtime with a colleague called Geoff, to 'babysit' a new system that was going in. We were supposed to test it over the weekend so that when the operators around the country came to use it on Monday morning it actually worked. There was some technical problem however, and we discovered it was going to take hours for a 'database restore' to run. It seemed the best thing to do was just sleep at the office on Saturday night and start testing at 6 a.m. on the Sunday morning, when the restore would have been completed. So, that is exactly what we did.

Geoff and I slept on the office floor that night, on the 4th floor of 207 Old Street. We gave the poor security guard the fright of his life when he saw our bodies curled up on the floor as he did his rounds at 3 a.m. The result of this dedication meant that I received the maximum performance rise of 6% and early promotion. This wasn't my first promotion. At 21 I'd got a 10% rise and was well on my way up the corporate ladder. I was responsible for a team of five other people, which seemed a step in the right direction, although I have to admit that after just a few weeks of having so much extra responsibility I was tempted to give BT my 10% back and return to my old job!

By my late 20s I'd reached the dizzy heights of management. I'd really made it; at least that's what Mum thought! My job title was 'Customer Relationship Management Systems Programme Manager'. It sounded quite impressive, I suppose, but what did this title really mean? The truth was it obliged me to go to an awful lot of meetings that were incredibly dull. Frustratingly, despite my fairly grand job title, I had precious little power to make any changes and I was often hamstrung by red tape, something I had discovered early on that huge corporations like BT tend to have in abundance. I'll give you an example of just how much red tape there was, and how irritating it was to me. One time, when my computer mouse stopped working, I had to get not one but three senior managers to sign off its replacement! If I hadn't already started to go bald, I'm sure I'd have been tearing my hair out!

Guess what? Somehow, the whole job wasn't fun any more. I now had stress and pressure, staff to manage, policies and standards to follow and no end of office politics to endure. Let me tell you, it can be pretty demoralising putting all your efforts into delivering a project and then, after six months of solid effort, being told that very same project had just been scrapped! This happened many times to me at BT and definitely had an effect on my job satisfaction and motivation. I plodded on though, because this was my chosen career, and it was a job for life, wasn't it? That's what I believed back then, so I kept my head down, continued to work hard and basically resigned myself to the fact that work was work and I just had to get on with it. I had bills to pay and I was earning decent money, so what choice did I have? Eventually I had 120 staff under me and my neck was on the block if I didn't deliver the systems on time. It was incredibly stressful, but that was what I'd signed up for so I just had to carry on, didn't I?

LESSON TIME! Simon Says:

Don't wait until you fall down an escalator to ask yourself the question 'What am I doing here and what is life about?' Ask yourself that question TODAY.

Whether you're a school-leaver or not, ask yourself what you REALLY want to do with your life. Are you making choices based on the expectations of people around you, or on what you actually want to do? Explore all your options and don't get sucked into following a path you feel you ought to take.

Don't regret any jobs you have done – even if you hated your boss or the company you worked for, you will ALWAYS have learned some valuable lessons along the way. Think about what these are – maybe write a list. It will probably be longer than you think and will help you if you do become an Interpreneur like me.

CASE STUDY

Keith Franklyn

Cpc4you.co.uk

cpc-training.net

I had been a haulage contractor running my own smallish business for over 30 years and, as I was not getting any younger and the business was more running me then me running the business, I was looking for a way to move on to something less stressful.

Around this time I received an invitation to Andrew Reynolds' Bootcamp in Bournemouth and I wondered if an Internet business would be the answer. I went along and one of the speakers on stage at that bootcamp was Simon, who I found to be very motivational and someone who talked a lot of sense. I immediately related to him and when he said that he was looking to take some students on and take them by the hand to start an Internet business I immediately signed up for his training course, at a cost of £1,997.

I was 61 years old at the time and in our appraisal talk Simon asked what were my interests. 'All I know is haulage,' I said, so we worked on that.

We developed a Certificate of Professional Competence home training course to enable you to obtain your CPC in Road Haulage to operate HGV vehicles. This comprised of a physical manual, 380 pages long, an audio CD covering 32 items and two data CDs covering past exam papers with questions and answers and mock exams.

Simon showed me how to set up websites, a shopping cart, autoresponders, Google marketing and everything necessary to go live on the Internet. In the first month of trading I made £3,500, which more than covered the investment in Simon for his tuition.

Move on to October 2016 and I have now followed his advice to 'Rinse and Repeat', so now I also supply a course for Public Service Vehicles PSV (Buses & Coaches). We keep all the information up to date with the current regulations and transport laws, together with the latest exam papers. Besides that there is very little effort involved, other then dispatching the orders. As this is an 'evergreen product', with new people coming into transport all the time, I can't see this changing.

As a conservative estimate I've made at least £135,000 profit with this business. The beauty is it is takes up very little of my time and is run from my home in Waltham Abbey, Essex. It was exactly what I was looking for when I first met Simon and was looking to change my work and my life.

All I can say is 'a very big thank you Simon' for tremendous help in those early days, which has given me a much better lifestyle and enabled me to purchase a property in Spain to enjoy my retirement.

If anyone is looking for a mentor to change their lifestyle they need look no further than Simon Coulson.

CHAPTER 2

Fake It Til You
Make It

As a kid I loved listening to music and mum encouraged me to learn an instrument. My granddad played in a brass band and he appeared one day with a cornet for me to try learning, but I didn't progress very far. Then I tried the guitar after my mum fixed me up with some lessons with a guy called Michael Archer, a talented musician who lived in our street. This didn't last for more than a few weeks, and I think the reason for this was that I was actually more interested in playing the piano.

At a young age my nan's next-door neighbour had given us an old piano that he didn't have room for any more. I used to sit there trying to play it - somewhat unsuccessfully - and my mum picked up on this and signed me up for lessons, firstly at my school and then with a succession of local piano teachers. I'm ashamed to say this too was to no avail. I went along to a handful of lessons, failed dismally to do any productive practise at home and really just wasn't in to it all. Looking back now I can see why. In those days piano teachers taught classical music only, which meant it was all Bach, Mozart and Beethoven. This wasn't the music I liked so I had no interest in playing it. At the time I was much more into 80s icons such as Nik Kershaw and Howard Jones, and I loved bands like Duran Duran and The Human League.

At the piano lessons I found there was a steep learning curve with understanding the musical notation, and I think the biggest problem I had was that I had no idea what the classical music I was being taught was supposed to sound like. I'd be given a piece of music – all lines and dots on a sheet - and try to practise it, but as I had no reference point for what it was meant to sound like I couldn't tell if my efforts were right or wrong, which was frustrating and demoralising. These days I expect it's much easier with iPads and YouTube and so on to help kids learn, and I'm sure piano teachers today teach music that's not hundreds of years old (at least I hope not). Anyhow, that was my unfortunate experience of piano lessons. I only stuck at them for a few weeks and never even got to the first rung on the musical ladder to achieve a 'Grade 1'.

Nonetheless, my interest in playing was not forgotten. Once I was earning decent money at BT I treated myself to an electronic keyboard, which was a fantastic Roland Juno 2 synthesizer. I bought it on a bit of a whim and didn't know how to play it of course, but it made some great noises and it was fun to have a go. Sometimes I'd listen to a track on the radio and try to figure out how to play the song by ear but it was pretty hit and miss, and not surprisingly the music I managed to make was not of a very high standard at all. After a few months I lost interest and my synthesizer found its way onto the top of the wardrobe and started to gather dust.

However, at the age of 25 I went on holiday over New Year to the Canary Islands, where I really enjoyed watching the live band at the hotel every night. I was inspired, and that was it. I decided my New Year's resolution was going to be to join a band on my return to the UK. As luck would have it, in the week I was back from holiday I was reading the local free ads newspaper when an advert caught my eye. *'5-piece rock/pop band playing originals and covers seeks keyboard player to complete line-up. Influences Crowded House, The Who, Paul Weller'* it read.

I called the number straightaway and found the band rehearsed at the Red Lion pub in Northfleet on Tuesday evenings, which was close to where I lived. I was invited to come along for an audition, which I was really pleased about, even though at this point I couldn't actually play one complete song on my Roland Juno 2. In fact, all I could do was play the intro to Elton John's 'Your Song' (badly, I might add), and that was the highlight of my repertoire. Even worse, I normally just plugged this keyboard into my hi-fi at home but of course that was no good for playing in a band in a pub. I got around this by borrowing a pair of disco speakers from a friend, and a hi-fi separates amplifier from another friend, before pitching up at the Red Lion for my audition.

The guys in the band seemed nice enough. Gary Gee was on vocals (such a cool name, I thought), a guy called Steven was on the bass, Richard was on the guitar and Tim was on the drums. After I plugged in they asked me what I could play and so I demonstrated my poor intro to Elton's number, coming to a halt about eight bars in. After an embarrassing silence Gary said: 'OK, let's do 'The One I Love' by R.E.M, this one's in E minor. I gulped. *'This one's in E minor' – what the hell does that mean?'* I had absolutely no idea. A crushing realization came over me that I was well out of my depth, and I wished the ground could just open up and swallow me to save me from further embarrassment. My saving grace was the whole band was playing this together, so I turned down the volume on my keyboard to ensure nobody could hear any of the random noises coming out of it, then I mimed along with the guys.

At the end of that song I hoped I'd be excused and would never bump into any of these band members ever again. Not so! 'OK, let's do 'Weather With You' in D' Gary said. This excruciating ordeal went on for almost three hours and my nerves were shredded. *Surely they must realise I haven't got a clue here?* At the end of the night I packed my gear back into the car, dying of embarrassment about the whole experience and just wanting to disappear as quickly as possible. I was just about to drive off when Gary called out 'Same time next week Simon?'. I don't know why given the state I was in but, before I could engage my brain, my voice piped up 'Yes, sure'. What on earth had I done?

So, that's the story of how I came to be in a band. I had a sharp learning curve ahead of me, and I realised the first thing I had to do was to decode the language the guys were using. I needed to know what all this 'in A major, Bsus4, Dsus2, F sharp minor' meant, because at that point in time it was all gobbledegook to me, despite the various music lessons I'd attempted as a child. My response to this was to go out and buy a book on music theory. I did this in my lunch break from BT, walking to the nearest music shop at the Barbican Centre and purchasing 'Grade 1 Music Theory' – a delightful pink book, as I remember.

I started studying my music theory book very carefully and I gradually learned from it. At the same time I went along to the Red Lion every

Tuesday to practise with the guys, taking with me a notebook and pen to write down the chords. I still couldn't play, but I asked the other band members to tell me what the chords were in each part of the song. That way I was slowly learning the basics of music and managing to busk along. My contribution at that stage was just a simple string or organ sound in a one-handed chord for each bar – basically using one hand to play three notes – just to fatten up the sound a bit. I didn't perform in public with the band to begin with, but after about six months Gary and the guys decided I was ready to be seen with them. I think this decision was taken on the basis the random noises I contributed finally added more to their music than they took away!

I eventually went on to play in In The Red, as the band was called, for a couple of years. Over this time period I became a very basic but competent keyboard player. In The Red eventually split, so I joined another band, called The Cold Tuesdays. This next group of guys was generally a bit more skilful and they had a larger repertoire, so playing with them every week made me raise my game a bit higher still. I really enjoyed the challenge and I looked forward to every gig. I'd heard the expression 'fake it 'til you make it' and I guess you could say that's exactly what I did with the band every week.

We rarely got more than £100 for a gig between us. With anything up to seven band members, and after deducting essential expenses such as petrol and bar bills, invariably we were actually paying for the pleasure of being in the band. I wasn't bothered about this. I'd discovered something I truly loved doing; playing with the band and entertaining others gave me a real buzz. I certainly wasn't getting a buzz in my day job at BT any longer: I'd been there for about a decade by now and I certainly wasn't feeling inspired or fulfilled by my role and the corporate lifestyle I was leading.

Incidentally, many years later I asked Gary and the boys why they had given me my first band job when I clearly had no clue or talent. 'Of course we realised you had no clue,' they told me, 'but you seemed liked an alright guy so we thought you might learn. Besides, we'd been running that ad for six months and you were the first guy who ever applied!' So there you have it – I benefited from the basic principle of supply and demand. The lack of supply of keyboard players essentially made me a much more valuable commodity than I ever could have imagined!

In 2002, when I was aged 31 and had been playing in bands for about five or six years, I went to see a new, up and coming band called Coldplay perform at the Brighton Centre. They had just released their second major album, *A Rush Of Blood To The Head,* and I was blown away by their performance that night. On the drive home up the motorway a thought struck me. *Wouldn't it be fantastic to start a tribute band to Coldplay?* If you're not familiar with the concept of a tribute band, it's basically a band that plays the songs of a famous band and typically calls itself a name that is relevant to the band they are paying tribute to. Even back then there were plenty of these bands around the country, often performing on the corporate cabaret circuit or at weddings and other functions, like graduation parties.

My mind went into overdrive. I imagined there was plenty of work out there for the right tribute band. I loved Coldplay's music, and it was a band that was certainly on the up, so surely a Coldplay tribute band would be a popular success? Even though I was only a keyboard player I harboured dreams of singing in a band, and now I started to imagine myself not just being a mute musician at the back, but joining in with the singing too. If it worked out, maybe the guys and me could earn more than £100 a gig? More importantly, maybe we might get to perform to a bigger crowd than the maximum of about 50 we were used to playing to, and we might even get gigs that weren't all within 10 miles of my house in Gravesend!

The next day I called a few musician friends I'd played with over the years and got them interested in joining me on this project. In the end there was Rick McMunn on drums, Dan Slowly on bass and Steve Jenner on guitar. I'd only played keyboards with these guys before, and in fact they will tell you that over the years I'd positively REFUSED to have a microphone anywhere near me to even do a few backing vocals. Now I was suddenly telling them I not only wanted to sing as well as play keyboards, but I wanted to create a brand new tribute band. Coolplay was the name I came up with. In hindsight the guys were very good. They could have laughed or dismissed my idea as a bit of a mad fantasy, but thankfully they were all really supportive and open-minded, and they agreed to give it a try. I guess that is another lesson learned: when you have nothing to lose, why not give something a try?

The four of us spent several months learning most of the songs on Coldplay's two albums until we got our renditions to an acceptable standard. Of course Coldplay's music was quite cleverly arranged and required a bit more effort from the band compared with the pop 'standards' we were all used to covering on the pub circuit. Anyhow we mastered it and in 2003 Coolplay was ready to be unleashed on the British public.

Our first gig was just for friends, which is probably just as well. I've still got the video and looking back I have to say it was pretty dire! Nevertheless, I think we were the ONLY tribute band to Coldplay at the time, and what's more they were becoming big news and getting increasingly popular. Slowly but surely Coolplay started getting some good gigs, playing events such as university graduation balls with an audience of 2000+, and a pay packet for the band of around £2,000 between us. In fact, our third ever gig was one such graduation ball and saw us sharing the bill with the Appleton sisters (formerly of the hit band All Saints) and Lisa Maffia. It wasn't exactly A-List, but for a newly formed band like us this was really pretty exciting. Funnily enough, I can remember that we kept the towels used by the Appleton sisters as a trophy for the following few months, until we had them stolen by an enthusiastic fan in Birmingham! On another gig our warm-up act was Limahl from 80s band Kajagoogoo. As a kid I remember watching him on *Top Of The Pops* and now suddenly he was our support act! It was all good fun. Suddenly our audiences had gone up 50-fold, our wages 20-fold and we were being inundated with offers of gigs.

My idea had certainly worked and the tribute band was paying off and getting busier, but unfortunately there was an annoying fly in the ointment: I still had my day job with BT to work around. The gigs were mostly at the weekend and so I could manage to juggle the two jobs, but to be honest BT was becoming a bit of a constraint. I wasn't enjoying the job at all any more – I'd been there for 13 years - and I wished I could devote more of my time to the band. Having had it ingrained in me for years that I was doing the right thing in having a steady job with a big corporation, it took me a little while to 'think outside the box', but the penny eventually dropped – or perhaps it would be more accurate to say that I dropped.

It was around this time that I collapsed at King's Cross and found myself questioning how I ended up in a heap on the floor at the bottom of the escalator, and wondering what the hell was I doing with my life for it to have come to this. After that it really didn't take a genius to work things out. Perhaps I didn't have to work for BT after all! Perhaps I had made a mistake ever going down that 'job for life' route in the first place? I'd finally found what I loved doing, and that was music. Thanks to the success of Coolplay I could earn as much from two gigs as it would take me a whole week to earn at BT, commuting from Monday to Friday and putting in long hours. I didn't want to rely on the band as my only source of income, as I had no idea how long Coolplay would be in demand, but while I had this opportunity why didn't I leave BT and do something else that fitted around my music better?

LESSON TIME! Simon Says:

Don't ignore what your heart is telling you. After failing to play the cornet, guitar and piano, my future as a musician appeared to be over before it began! My heart told me something different though – so hold on to your dreams and be true to yourself.

Read local papers as much as you can. There are all kinds of opportunities lurking in their pages, and you never know where they might lead you.

Go to Interpreneur.com/resources to get extra materials and free Internet Marketing training

Fortune favours the brave, so when an opportunity arises, ask yourself 'What have I got to lose?' rather than worrying about all the things that could go wrong.

When you feel out of your depth you have two choices – let yourself sink or choose to swim. ALWAYS choose to swim, and use all the aids you can, whether that means taking classes, buying books, enrolling on a course or simply picking the brains of a friend, colleague or mentor who can help.

When you feel inspired and excited, you are probably onto something. Don't ignore your gut feelings, don't be afraid to brainstorm with friends you trust, and don't have pre-conceived ideas about how your suggestions might be received – often you'll be pleasantly surprised!

Enjoy being in the moment. When Coolplay started getting bigger and bigger gigs we had no idea how far we could go as a band, but what we did know was that we were enjoying ourselves HERE AND NOW.

When you have a wake-up call – whether it's a health scare or some other defining moment in your life – DO NOT IGNORE IT. Remember the phrase 'every cloud has a silver lining' and make positive changes rather than feeling defeated or simply trying to pick up the pieces and muddle on.

CASE STUDY

Bob Cuthbertson

loyaltyspace.com

I first met Simon almost nine years ago at a Heathrow hotel where I did one of his weekend courses that introduced me to AdWords and SEO. During the course I set up my first WordPress website which, with the help of constructive AdWords, placed my site on top of the search engines for 'Loyalty Card Systems'.

As a direct result of the Adwords campaign I started to attract business including; restaurants, hair salons, hotels, retail outlets and beauty salons. One of the beauty companies was Clarins UK, based in London – amazing when you consider the cost of the AdWord which attracted Clarins UK to venture onto our site was £1.50. This resulted in a phone call from their marketing department to invite me to a presentation and I went to their head office to present our product.

Clarins UK chose our solution to replace their paper card loyalty system, upgrading to the 'Smart Card' solution with handheld smart card terminals. The roll-out commenced with an initial order of £50,000 worth of smart cards and the first 50 terminals for a further £35,000. Over the next year the order increased to another 50 terminals, being supplied to; Selfridges, John Lewis, Debenhams, Beatties and other well-known stores. In total Clarins ordered over 350,000 cards over a four-year period and theirs became one of the largest loyalty schemes running in the UK.

Clearly this business and others changed my lifestyle dramatically and put my family in a position to enjoy luxuries we had not experienced before. I'm 64 now, and we were able to pay for private education for my daughter (which was life-changing for her) and pay a chunk off our mortgage on our home in Beverley, East Yorkshire.

If I had not attended Simon's courses and not taken his team's advice, nor implemented an AdWords strategy and built my WordPress website during that weekend course I would, without doubt, not have picked up the business from the Internet.

Throughout the years I have continued to purchase *Internet Business School* products and attended follow-up courses to keep up to date with this fast-changing Internet world. Today we are still using all of Simon's strategies and we still receive leads from the Internet, which is our main source of income. Every business needs inspiration to get started, and through attending the *Internet Business School* courses you will certainly have many things to think about. The hands-on experience was exciting and rewarding.

I wish Simon all the best with this book. He has helped many individuals and businesses and so is deserving of recognition and all his success.

CHAPTER 3

Leaving
The Rat Race

Luckily for me, in the late summer of 2003, BT was shedding staff. A big redundancy scheme was put in place and I saw my chance and grabbed it immediately. There was a possibility I might lose my job before too long anyhow - during my time at BT staff levels had been greatly reduced and all the signs were that this trend would continue. It was time to get out on my own terms, so I applied for voluntary redundancy and thankfully got what I wanted. I left in December 2003 feeling like a weight had been lifted from my shoulders when I walked out of the office for the very last time.

Besides playing in the band I didn't have much of a plan, other than figuring that as most of our gigs were on a Friday and Saturday I would have plenty of time to find some other job or business to get involved in. I had no idea what this might be but I wasn't worried. My redundancy pay was almost £20,000. I looked at my outgoings and thought I could probably cut back on my expenses, which would help to keep the pressure off until I found a new day job. I didn't need to earn as much money as I was on at BT, as all the time I was 'corporate man' I was spending on things I didn't really need. Also, I had the band money to keep me afloat which was a big help too.

I worked out that with a bit of careful spending, and as long as the Coolplay gigs kept coming in, I could probably eke out a living for a least a year, and that was plenty of time to re-plan my life. I fully expected to be taking another job after a year at the most, when I estimated the redundancy money would have completely run out. I was under no illusions about the band's ongoing success. I knew that Coldplay would not be the flavour of the month forever, therefore Coolplay offered me no guarantees whatsoever for the future, so I'd certainly have to have some other 'regular' job alongside my music.

My decision to walk away from my 'job for life' that I'd had for 14 years provoked a few difficult conversations. My mum and some of my friends and work colleagues thought, quite frankly, I'd lost the plot. I'd had a job with a major company and what's more it was a job that paid well. What was I thinking? My basic salary had risen to over £60,000 and the package included private healthcare, a company

BMW convertible, bonus scheme, share options and more. I think the people around me might have understood my decision better had my answer to their question 'What are you going to do now?' not been met with a shrug and a 'Dunno'.

In fairness, apart from questioning me and saying they thought I was stupid, short-sighted or crazy, no one actually tried that hard to stop me quitting my job. I probably wouldn't have listened anyway and I guess they knew that. I think they could see I was probably in danger of becoming completely burnt out at BT, they could equally see the passion I had for music and how much pleasure I got from being in the band.

One really useful exercise I did as I finalised my decision to leave BT was to have a long, hard look at my expenses. I'd urge you to think about this too. For each expense ask yourself if you REALLY need it, or could you scale it back or even eradicate it completely?

Looking at my expenses back in 2003, I decided there were a few things I could definitely get rid of. For example, I had a top-rate satellite TV Package. Could I live without it? Of course – it was gone! I had vehicle breakdown cover, again a top of the range package, but I hadn't used it for years. The bass player in the band was a mechanic and I knew he would help out if I ever broke down, so that was gone too. I looked at my bills and found I spent an average of £50 - £100 a month on clothes for work. My BT job required suits, shirts, ties, shoes – all those things I wouldn't need any more of, at least for the time being while I worked out what I was doing next.

After making all of those sensible cost-cutting measures, I did something a little less wise. When I got my redundancy cheque for almost £20,000 I decided to invest a large chunk of it in a van for the band. My thinking was that I needed a car to get around in, as the company BMW had gone back, and if I was going to spend more time on the band I felt we needed something a bit more professional-looking than the four separate cars we normally arrived in for gigs.

I shopped around and found there was this fantastic MPV import from Japan called a Toyota Granvia. It looked quite modern and it cost me about £15,000. It was a great vehicle, and bearing in mind the old company BMW convertible was worth a lot more than this and was a far more prestigious brand, nevertheless I much preferred the MPV. It was a four-wheel drive with five seats and most importantly it had room to fit a drum kit, keyboard, guitars and amps. It wasn't new but it had air-conditioning and features you didn't even get on the BMW, like electric curtains on every window. You gotta love the Japanese! As we'll learn later, that van was to rack up some miles over the next few years.

I vividly remember the journey home from work on my last day with BT. After leaving the office and feeling the weight lifting from my shoulders I'd had a final drink with my old work colleagues. They looked somewhat bewildered that I was actually leaving yet didn't know what I was doing next. Somehow, I wasn't bewildered at all, and nor was I afraid in any way. Instead I was quietly optimistic that something would turn up.

On the way home I had to stop and get some petrol. Whilst in the queue I noticed a little revolving bookstand with a somewhat limited range of books on display. One of them caught my eye, it was entitled *The Beermat Entrepreneur*. Somehow that seemed kind of appropriate. I was certainly ready to be some kind of entrepreneur, and with the band I was likely to be hanging round a lot of places with beermats, so I added that to the Galaxy and Redbull I'd already picked up in the shop. (I've often wondered if petrol stations deliberately don't employ enough staff to maximise upsells while we queue! And by the way, I don't remember picking up any life-changing tips from that particular book – but at least it got me thinking along the right lines about being some kind of entrepreneur!)

Driving home I didn't feel at all perturbed at what lay in front of me. As I put more distance between myself and my old office – my old life – I began to feel not just calm and optimistic, but liberated and excited. It was a massive relief to have finally broken free from the corporate rat race, and although I didn't know what I was going to do next I was really looking forward to it. My laid-back behaviour seems strange to me now, considering I didn't know where that next pay cheque was coming from. I was trading down my luxury car for a van, cancelling my satellite TV and other stuff I'd got used to, but somehow I felt great - almost euphoric.

I guess it had started to dawn on me that those material things DON'T actually make happiness, and that you can be happier without them. Above all I was delighted to be free of all the pressure that goes with a managerial job in a big corporation. I didn't have to think any more about doing the office '9-5' every day, or about being responsible for the actions of other people who worked under me. Nor did I have to worry about delivering large projects to time and on budget. Most importantly, I was no longer accountable to others for everything I did at work. I had freedom and even before I'd put my key in the front door that night I was asking myself why I hadn't done this years before. Of course, this was still before all the good stuff that happened had actually started to unfold, but even then I was happier in myself. I'd cut off the corporate chains and I was in charge of my own destiny.

One of the big lessons I learned that day was that sometimes what seems scary isn't nearly half as scary when you actually just do it. It's the decision itself that creates the feelings of fear, but having made the choice you have taken the plunge, expunged the fear and then you can start to wonder what all the fuss was about. As you're going to read about in subsequent chapters, one thing I have learnt and completely taken to heart is that we only get one go at this business called life. It is not a dress rehearsal, and it's important to enjoy your life and be fulfilled, every day. If you are stuck in a rut and are maybe trapped in a job you're not happy with, then only YOU can change that, and in my opinion we all owe it to ourselves to make those changes. Sometimes you just have to have the confidence to take the decision to set about some important changes in your life – and sometimes they don't even have to be that big.

LESSON TIME! Simon Says:

It can be scary giving up a stable income, but make a list of all the money you will SAVE simply by NOT doing a 9-5 job. This will include obvious things like work clothes, lunches in the staff canteen, travel costs and so on. There will be less obvious costs too – for instance, you might want to add take-aways, a dog walker, a cleaner, car washes etc. to the list, as these are only 'necessities' because of the hours you work and are away from home. All of this will probably mount up to a surprisingly tidy sum that you will be able to offset against your loss of a guaranteed income.

Similarly, list ALL of your general outgoings and expenses, and work out what other savings you can make in addition to those work-related expenses. This is usually a positive exercise as there are always expenses you can remove straightaway that you won't even miss (like expensive TV bundles or gold standard car breakdown packages).

Don't worry about what other people think, because no matter what choices you make you will always have naysayers and detractors who will try to put you off.

I remember a quote from Atticus Finch in *To Kill a Mockingbird* - 'You never really understand a person until you consider things from his point of view . . . until you climb inside of his skin and walk around in it'. Only YOU know how you feel about your life and how you want to change it. Follow your heart.

Don't do what I did and buy a depreciating asset with your precious redundancy money! I loved the Toyota Granvia, but spending £15,000 on it was pretty silly.

Stay positive and believe in yourself, even when you have no idea how things will pan out. There's a much better chance you'll succeed if you BELIEVE you will.

Don't let fear hold you back – what seems scary isn't nearly half as scary when you actually just do it.

Remember, LIFE IS NOT A DRESS REHEARSAL!

Go to Interpreneur.com/resources to get extra materials and free Internet Marketing training

CASE STUDY

Maciej Banaszkiewicz

MagVolcano.com

Since my early teens I have always wanted to run my own business, but I was brought up to believe that going to university and getting the 'right' job was the way to succeed in life. I did just this – eventually doing an internship at the Marriot Hotel in Washington DC – and then I got a steady, well-paid job for a large hotel group based in London. Having achieved this I was meant to be 'living the dream' but I wasn't. After two years I felt burned out, depressed and had no clear vision what to do.

One of my responsibilities at work was to make sure the events put on in the hotel were running smoothly. One day in 2008 a person called Simon Coulson was running an event about Internet marketing. I knew what the Internet and marketing were but had no clue about Internet marketing, and to be honest I was quite sceptical about the whole 'working from home' idea, which I knew was part of Simon's talk.

Afterwards I spoke to the attendees. Some told me that this was not the first time they had attended one of Simon's events, and that Simon's teachings had transformed their lives.

I decided to give it a go and enrolled myself onto one of Simon's weekend seminars. It was overwhelming at first, but by the end of the first day I felt like I was equipped with some secret wizard's knowledge! I couldn't wait to try out all of the stuff I had learned and I took action immediately – throwing myself into everything from SEO and eBay trading, to selling ebooks, affiliate marketing and setting up membership sites.

I didn't have to wait long to reap great rewards. Affiliate marketing alone was bringing me £10,000 a month – 3x the money I was getting from my 'right' job - and the best part was that I was working from home. Eventually I left the hotel job and dedicated myself full-time to my own business, which was what I always dreamed of.

Currently I run a few businesses including a creative design agency, several magazines available as apps, and I run an Internet-based platform for making mobile apps. My latest creation is *MagVolcano.com,* where we help business owners and experts to increase their profits and gain exposure. We achieve all of that by creating, publishing and managing mobile apps for them.

I would like to take this opportunity and thank Simon for opening my eyes and showing me that there is more in life than the hustle and bustle of a regular, steady job. I strongly recommend the seminars and the school Simon runs. My life is transformed and the corporate burn-out I experienced is, thankfully, a distant memory.

CHAPTER 4

Where Is Bulgaria?

Now I was unemployed. Apart from the regular weekend gigs with the band booked in the diary I still had no idea where the long-term money was going to come from.

Once my redundancy date had been confirmed I had started paying more attention to the 'Business Opportunities' sections of ads in newspapers, and I'd seen a classified ad in a newspaper selling a set of DVDs about how to make money from home. I bought a set for £67, it was put together by an American businessman and sold by someone called Andrew Reynolds, who due to my purchase now had my contact details on file.

Very shortly after this I got an invitation to a workshop Andrew was putting on in London, which was all about learning how to start your own business from home. This was only about a week after I'd left BT, and in the absence of any better ideas about what I was going to do when I wasn't gigging, I decided to book myself a place and go along.

The seminar was a real eye-opener. Andrew told us his business model and explained how he made literally millions from selling 'information products', mostly licensed from America. To be honest I was a bit of a cynic when I walked in the room, my gut reaction was to try to find the hole in what he was offering. *Surely if it was that simple, everybody would be doing this? What was the catch?* Those were the questions that went through my head as I listened to the seminar.

Then Andrew passed around some bank statements showing that he currently had over £1 million cash sitting in his current account. I'd seen plenty of bank accounts when I was younger. As well as helping out with my dad's accountancy business in the school holidays, I'd worked in a bank for a few weeks at the age of 16 before deciding I hated it and wanted to stay at school and do A levels. However, none of that experience prepared me for what I was looking at now, as I had never seen a bank statement with anything like THIS amount of credit on it before! £1 million – it was incredible!

Suddenly the sceptical questions in my head were subsiding. I sat up and really started to take notice of what this guy was saying.

Andrew's business model was basically this:

1   Find a product that is available with resale rights. This would typically be a DVD set or CD set containing about 3 - 15 discs, usually sourced in America and brought to the UK, and nearly always some kind of information product

2   Get a copywriter to write a sales letter promoting the virtues of the product

3   Buy a postal mailing list

4   Print thousands of letters and post to everyone on the mailing list

5   Sit back and wait for the sales

Andrew gave examples of the types of training products you could licence:

• How to trade stock markets

• How to make money in property investment

• How to win at blackjack

• How to repair microwave ovens

It sounded simple enough and, judging by this guy's bank statement, it clearly worked. However, I was thinking to myself that this model meant you needed to shell out a lot of cash in order to get started. It could cost thousands to buy the license to resell the product, thousands more to pay a copywriter to write a sales letter and purchase a mailing list, and yet more money to cover the printing and postage of the mailshots. Realistically, this meant spending at least £5,000 before you earned a penny. This didn't sound ideal to me, but what I loved about the business model was that it took advantage of the fact information products have a high profit margin. The DVD and

CD sets were costing £5 - £10 to duplicate and ship but then selling for hundreds per set, often yielding 95% profit margins or more.

Unfortunately, after buying the band's 'tour bus' I had less than £5,000 of my redundancy money left, which was one of the reasons the start-up costs of this business model concerned me. My mum and other people around me had told me that I should be investing my redundancy money into the property market, and I had to agree that on paper this seemed an infinitely more sensible idea than buying a depreciating asset like a Japanese MPV, or possibly investing in the resale of information DVD and CDs. With under £5,000 in the bank I couldn't see any way of investing in the UK property market, but then an idea struck me. Could I invest in a property abroad, where prices were lower? Would that be a better bet than trying to sell an information product I'd have to invest my last few thousand pounds in?

I'd seen a lot in the newspapers around this time about emerging property markets in Europe, and in particular the Eastern European countries such as Bulgaria and Croatia. One newspaper article labelled Bulgaria 'the new Costa Del Sol' really caught my eye. I started doing some research online to learn more about the country. I didn't even know where Bulgaria was so I searched the Internet and found a map just to figure out where it was located in Europe. I could see it was neighbours with countries such as Greece and Turkey which were already mainstream European holiday and investment property locations, so that seemed like an encouraging sign. Next I read up online about the economics of the country, its politics and the cost of living and, most interesting of all, the fact that Bulgaria was joining the European Union (EU) on January 1st 2007. This meant property prices were predicted to rocket, so right now, in early 2004, was the perfect time to invest. The experts actually said that property was likely to quadruple as soon as Bulgaria joined the EU, so a 400% increase over two years seemed a good deal.

I had a friend who had also read about buying in Bulgaria and so we decided we might both like to invest there and planned a visit.

At the time I was quite busy with the band, and when it came to the crunch my friend ended up flying out to Bulgaria on his own. When he arrived he called me and said it was crazy: the price of property was incredibly cheap and Brits were queuing up at estate agents to buy houses. What's more the prices were going up almost daily.

Not wanting to miss out I told my friend I trusted his judgement and said I'd send him the money immediately to buy me a house, which I did. I chose it via a picture message (and these were not great quality in 2004!), and he purchased a three-bed detached house for me, with 2,000 square metres of land, all for just £4,600.

So, that was how I spent the remainder of my redundancy money, investing in a property I had never seen in a country I had never stepped foot in. This wasn't quite what my mum had had in mind when she'd urged me to do the sensible thing and invest in property! Once again my friends and other members of the family were sceptical about how I was spending my precious redundancy money, but when I started showing people photographs of my new Bulgarian house and told them how much it had cost, they started to change their tune and had lots of questions:

- Why did you buy there?

- Where is it?

- How easy was it to buy a property in Bulgaria?

These were questions I was asked repeatedly, and when I gave my answers I could see that my friends and family were coming round to the idea that maybe this was a good investment after all. In fact, many of them started asking me exactly how they could buy a house in Bulgaria too. I told them the property market there had already been growing at 23% per annum, and explained about the expectation that property prices would quadruple when Bulgaria joined the EU. This made them really sit up and take notice and word quickly began to spread amongst friends of friends and various family members. Before I knew it I'd become a bit of a walking advert for investing in

Bulgaria, and I was dishing out my knowledge and research to stacks of interested people, often several times a day.

It was at this point that I began to think about what I had learnt at the workshop on information products, and then another thought struck me. Rather than buying a license to a product and reselling it, why didn't I create an information product of my own? I bet you can't guess what subject I had in mind!

Clearly, I seemed to have discovered a sector of the market people were interested in learning more about, so why not create an information product, in the form of an ebook, about investing in property in Bulgaria? It's worth remembering at this point that I hadn't even been to Bulgaria and nor did I know any Bulgarians, but this didn't put me off. Of course I had to do some serious research, but I could do it, no problem.

The first thing I did was to map out which topics I should cover in my book. I brainstormed the questions others had asked me, and the questions that I had asked myself when I was thinking of investing in a property, and I researched all of these questions and queries on Google. This gave me a skeleton outline for the book, which looked like this:

1   Introduction to Bulgaria

2   Why invest in Bulgaria?

3   Facts and figures

4   Regions of Bulgaria

5   Travelling to Bulgaria

6   Cost of Living

7   Maps

8   The buying process

9 Where to buy from

10 Resource directory

Next, for each of these chapter headings, I set about researching that particular topic and finding out all I could just by using Google as my research tool. This was something that anyone could have done, but nobody had ever bothered to do.

Let's look at these chapter headings, then let me give you some insight into how I created my first information ebook.

Chapter 1 – **Introduction to Bulgaria**. This was just a general introduction to Bulgaria, in terms of where it was, and giving a general overview of the country. It was easy to find information on this topic across the Internet, so I just rewrote content that I found for free on a number of different sites.

Chapter 2 – **Why Invest In Bulgaria?** For this chapter I researched a range of economic data. When I say 'researched' what I really mean is that I typed the words 'why invest in Bulgaria?' into Google – it was that simple. I found much of the data on the Bulgarian government's own site, where there was plenty of information about the country's economy. For specific information on the property market I found various financial analysis and property industry reports that I carefully summarized.

Chapter 3 – **Facts and Figures.** The information for this chapter all came courtesy of the American government. There is a website called the CIA World Factbook, which has all sorts of information about every country in the world. (cia.gov/library/publications/the-world-factbook/) This extremely useful site contains information about demographics, communication, infrastructure, government, population, climate, religion and more. Best of all, this information is all in the public domain, which means that anyone is free to take it and use it exactly as is, with no fear of copyright infringement.

Chapter 4 – **Regions of Bulgaria**. I used this chapter to provide information describing the different geographic regions of Bulgaria, so that someone thinking of investing in Bulgaria could consider the distinct parts of the country and what they offered. For instance, the country has beach resorts, ski resorts, historic towns and so on. These were factors to think about, as well as how long the holiday season lasted and what the occupancy was for different times of year. All of this was easily put together with a little help from the Bulgaria Tourism Board site, which had huge amounts of information about all of the regions, places to visit and so on.

Chapter 5 – **Travelling to Bulgaria**. This chapter covered how to get to Bulgaria through the basic four transport mechanisms – air, sea, rail and road. I simply used Google to find how you could travel to the country. For example, for air travel I looked up which UK airports you could fly from, using which airlines, and found out the frequency, cost and length of flights. For driving I looked at how you could drive across Europe, through which countries and where you might stop along the way.

Chapter 6 – **Cost of Living.** For this chapter I analysed the cost of living in Bulgaria. In reality all I did was research basic foodstuffs, such as bread, milk and eggs, and put together a table showing costs in the UK versus those in Bulgaria. I also compared costs of basic services and taxes such as electricity.

Chapter 7 – **Maps**. This was another easy chapter to pull together. The CIA World Factbook (above) had a collection of maps of the country that were public domain, so I quickly sourced those and added some links to some other free online map resources too.

Chapter 8 – **The Buying Process**. This was seemingly the hardest chapter of all to put together. Bulgaria had various laws and taxes relating to property purchase. For example, foreign nationals couldn't actually purchase a property directly in Bulgaria. The only way to make a purchase was by setting up a company in the country first, and then purchasing through the company. Having only purchased one property myself, and having my friend there to help me out, I was hardly an expert. Online information about this aspect of the book was a bit difficult to find too, and at this point I realised I needed a real expert to help with this chapter. I therefore contacted a few solicitors in Bulgaria who spoke English, and I found one who was willing to write this chapter for me. Instead of paying him a fee for this, the deal was that I would put his contact details at the end of this chapter, so that any readers who required an English-speaking solicitor could get in touch with him. This seemed a fair exchange and he was happy with this. The free advertising should bring him a steady stream of new clients, and all he had to do was write a few pages on the legal process for buying in Bulgaria.

Chapter 9 – **Where To Buy From**. This was simply a list of property agents that I found just using Google and some directory sites. Each property agent was listed with their contact details and website address. Incidentally, one of the estate agents listed contacted me and asked if their details could go in a box at the top of the list. I said I could do this for a fee of £2,000 – a figure I plucked out of the air. 'Great, where do we send the money?' they replied. Of course, this was a lesson learned and in the future I made a point of actively selling adverts instead of waiting for people to come knocking.

Chapter 10 – **Resource Directory.** This was just a list of all the websites I had used in the creation of the ebook, gathered in one place and neatly grouped in categories.

There are a few important things I should point out at this stage. The first thing is copyright. When putting together this ebook I was using information from a range of different sources. What you absolutely can't do (unless the source is public domain like the CIA World Factbook) is just 'cut and paste' the information you find straight into your product. What you need to do is find multiple sources of information on a topic and then rewrite this information in your own words, thus making it your own unique content. This takes a little bit of time but really isn't that onerous. If you really don't want to do this yourself you can outsource and give this job to someone else to write for you. The process is very similar to writing an essay or dissertation. Typically, you find lots of sources of information on a topic, write what you have read and researched in your own words, and then list all the people you 'borrowed' from and call it the bibliography or resource directory. It's really not that difficult. I could do it, and I don't mind admitting that I am someone who failed his English O level the first time around!

The entire process of researching and writing the *Bulgaria Property Guide* ebook took me around two weeks, or about 60 hours of work. Clearly it wasn't a five-minute job and it took some effort, but on the other hand it wasn't a massive investment of time considering I was building something that could potentially be a passive income earner for years to come.

Now I had created this ebook, the next thing I needed to do was start selling it. The business model I learned at that initial seminar about selling information products had involved huge costs in terms of buying mailing lists, paying a copywriter to write a sales letter and then sending out thousands of letters in the post. Another sales method I was taught at that seminar was to buy advertising space in national newspapers – again not cheap. So I looked around at other channels I could sell through, and I thought the Internet would be a perfect low-cost route to market.

I realised the first thing I needed was a website and a sales page to sell this ebook. I looked online and found some free tutorials on making simple web pages using something called 'HTML templates' and fortunately it all sounded a lot scarier than it actually turned out to be. Basically, you could go to a website, download a free website template and then edit the template on your own PC. At the time I used some software from Microsoft called 'Frontpage'. This worked in an almost identical way to Microsoft Word, which I had used before and was familiar with. So I got a free template and started writing the sales copy to sell the imaginatively titled *Bulgaria Property Guide*.

I'd never studied sales copy in my life, so I basically looked at some similar webpages that were selling guides on investing in places like

France, and just followed a similar structure. Effectively, all I really did was list the ten chapters in my book, and write a couple of sentences for each summarizing what people would find in that chapter. Then put a price on it of £17.95, which was a number I just picked out of the air based on similar prices I had seen for other information ebooks.

You can see a screen shot of how that sales page looked in the picture section. I registered a domain name for the website and used that simple piece of software Frontpage to upload my new website. The next thing I needed was some way to take payment from a customer when they bought my ebook. The easiest way to do this was using PayPal, which I already had an account with and was very easy to set up. I had only used PayPal to pay for goods up until now, so how did you take payment from other people? I discovered that within the 'Merchant Tools' section of my PayPal account was a section where you could generate the code to put a 'Buy Now' button onto your own website. I followed the instructions online and to my amazement easily created the button and added it to my page. And what's more it actually worked!

Now all I needed were customers! As all the sales were going through my website I somehow had to figure out how to get people to come and look at my page and hopefully be interested enough to buy my product. I knew most people used search engines to find websites, and Google was the dominant player in the UK marketplace, with around 70-80% of searches performed on it. I found there were two basic ways to get traffic from Google to your website. One was to pay for an advert which would appear on the right-hand margin of search results, and the other was to get Google to rank your website highly on the left-hand side (sometimes called natural or organic listings).

I started reading up about how search engines worked, and I quickly learned that basically everything revolved around 'keywords'. The concept was fairly simple. For any product or service being sold there is a set of keywords that people who are interested in that product or service are likely to look for. For example, in this market I was interested in people who were actively searching for phrases such as:

Go to Interpreneur.com/resources to get extra materials and free Internet Marketing training

- Bulgaria property

- Bulgaria investment

- Overseas property investment

- Buying property in Bulgaria

- Eastern European property

- Sofia property

- Black Sea property

To get your website ranked highly by Google, so that it listed on the left-hand side for each of these search phrases, required doing something called 'search engine optimisation' (SEO). I started reading up about this but it all sounded very complicated and time-consuming, and there also seemed to be lots of conflicting information out there about how best to achieve results. However, to get an advert listed on the right-hand side was easy. All you needed to do was:

1   Sign up with Google's AdWords scheme

2   Choose a list of keywords that you were interested in and that you would like to trigger your advert

3   Write a simple four-line advert

That all seemed fairly simple and a lot easier than 'search engine optimisation', so I chose this option and did it quite easily. Here is the amazing advert I ran:

Bulgaria Property Guide

Learn about all aspects of investing

In Bulgarian Property

bulgaria-property.org

The way that pricing works for Google AdWords is that you pay for results. In other words, you don't pay to run the advert; you simply pay an amount of money when somebody clicks on it. The 'cost per click' (CPC) depends on the level of competition in the market you are in. In simple terms, Google effectively auctions the advertising space, giving the highest spots to the highest bidder. As this was a new market with low competition, I found I could get clicks for as little as 2p per click. This meant that to get 100 'qualified' or relevant, interested visitors to my website would only cost me £2.

Did it work? Yes it did! I found that for every 100 visitors from Google AdWords I was making 2 sales on average. This is known as a 2% conversion rate, which was great. It meant I was spending £2 and generating sales of 2 x £17.95, or £35.90.

Within days I was selling 20 or more of these ebooks per day, all for £17.95 per electronic copy. Almost accidentally, I had created my first Internet cash machine, generating around £400 a day on autopilot.

So, my first foray into Internet marketing had been a big success. I didn't really know what I was doing at the start, but by learning a few simple rules and discovering some basic tools I had joined up the dots and created something that was making more than my old day job did. What's more, I had achieved all this within just a few weeks of leaving BT. In fact, in my very first month after taking my redundancy I generated over £10,000, and all from me reading a newspaper article about Bulgaria and spotting a hot niche in the market.

I decided I quite liked this Internet marketing thing and was going to look into how else I could use it to make even more money. I made a mental note to read more newspapers and look around for more hot trends, because if I'd done it once, I was confident I could do it again.

LESSON TIME! Simon Says:

Read all the sections in a newspaper - you never know what you will find. I can't stress this enough - if I hadn't read the classified ads I would not have gone to the seminar that set me on my journey.

Go to Interpreneur.com/resources to get extra materials and free Internet Marketing training

When you go to a 'how to make money' kind of seminar BE SCEPTICAL. Ask to see evidence the speaker has made money – you need proof, like a bank statement. There are four other questions you should also consider: are they teaching current methods? Can you learn from them, and by this I mean can they teach you in a way you will understand? Have they proved they had made it happen for others? Are they honest or are they offering some kind of magic button? Trust your instincts - if it sounds too good to be true, it probably is.

Don't let anyone over-complicate things and don't be daunted. There are actually only three things you need to make money on the Internet:

1 – Something to sell: a product or service

2 – Somewhere to sell from: your website

3 – Someone to sell to: SEO traffic, customers

All you need to know is how to make those three steps work BRILLIANTLY for you.

Don't think you have to take every piece of advice from a seminar – cherry-pick the bits that are useful to you and you might find you come up with your own winning formula.

LISTEN to what your friends and family are talking about – if they are interested in a topic or there is a buzz around a certain subject, maybe that is a market worth exploring.

Be confident in your ability. I never thought I could write a book of any kind, but when I started writing the ebooks I realised it was only like writing a series of short articles. The trick is to break it down into chapters and manageable chunks of text. Don't be overwhelmed – if I can do it you can! And look at me now, writing my life story!

Be aware of copyright infringement and plagiarism. Make sure material you are using is in the public domain. If you are using information from non-public domain sources you need to put it into your own words and credit your source in the bibliography.

CASE STUDY

Alex Buxton

getmyblackbelt.com

I did the 3-day marketing course in 2010 after seeing Simon speaking at a seminar. He blew my mind. If he could teach me so much in an hour, what could he teach me in three days?

I was 36 years old and already working in sales, but I wanted to create an 'automatic' source of income. At the start of the course we were told we would have a business up and running before the end of the three days so I was determined to come up with a business idea to give myself a head start.

I didn't have to look far. I was a black belt in karate and decided to make the best karate and self-defence DVD sets in the world.

Simon helped me with all the information I was lacking such as; how to master SEO, online payments, WordPress and much else besides. He also inspired me to see my plans through to fruition.

Within two days of launching my first product I was already making sales. Currently, my *140 Combat Moves* product is the best-selling self-defence DVD set in the UK and the second best-selling in the US. It has sold to all 50 US states and to most countries.

My *Get My Black Belt* business has spawned another enterprise called *Power Dragons (powerdragons.org)*, which I set up with the aim of helping disadvantaged pre-teens build life skills through martial arts. This has now been modified to meet the needs of all boys and girls aged 4-6, and I am looking to franchise this business out across the UK.

I have made tens of thousands of pounds from my DVD sets

and since making them four years ago I have done no work on *Get My Black Belt*. I'm based in Loudwater, Rickmansworth, and the money I earn from *Get My Black Belt* is all extra, passive income, running in the background - the money just comes in automatically. It means that if I want to book some intercontinental holidays, make home improvements or pay down the mortgage, I can just take the funds from Get My Black Belt.

Improving your lifestyle is not just about making money but giving back as well. Internet marketing skills are very highly sought after by charities and non-profits. I am keen on helping cheetahs and manage the websites of the Daniell Cheetah Project *(daniellcheetahproject.com)* and Cheetah Conservation Fund UK *(cheetah.org.uk)*. I have used online marketing to generate thousands of pounds of funds for both of them.

The return on investment from the training course with Simon was incredible and I am delighted I had the opportunity to participate in it. It is an opportunity not to be missed.

CHAPTER 5

Rinse And Repeat

So, my very first Internet project was up and running, and making over £400 a day on good days. The best part of this was the money came in every day without me having to do anything. The work had been done upfront writing the ebook, and whilst that had taken about 60 hours of research and compilation, now it was done I didn't have to do anything more to collect hundreds of pounds of profit every day. I was literally making money while I slept.

At this point I could have just sat on my butt and counted the money, but of course I thought what if I did another one of these ebooks, or even several? Maybe they could be successful too, and why settle for making £400 a day when you could be making £800, £1200 or £16,000? I was getting excited now, dreaming of building a string of 'Internet cash machines'. Even if I only built one a month, by the end of the year I'd have 12 income streams that could make me rich!

The question was how could I successfully repeat the success of the Bulgaria book? I certainly seemed to have struck gold on my first outing with a subject matter around overseas property investment. I remembered that little saying: 'if it ain't broke, don't fix it' and decided to follow that advice. Why not do exactly the same thing but for a different overseas property market? I figured there must be other places where investors were looking to buy property, and so I put my thinking cap on again.

A quick look at a European map told me that Croatia was just round the corner from Bulgaria. From keeping my ears and eyes open, reading the papers and doing a bit of basic research on Google I knew this was another emerging property market. Thus ebook number two came about, complete with my next imaginative title – the *Croatia Property Guide.* A few weeks later that one was done and dusted, and once again the money started dropping into my PayPal account on autopilot, completely hands free.

Naturally, the research for this second guide followed the same pattern as the first one, and I found it a lot easier to do second time round as I had now learnt the process. As soon as the Croatia ebook was up and running and making money I started thinking about other countries I could produce property investment guides on. I easily found a list of 20 possible countries, but it wasn't obvious which to do next. Bulgaria and Croatia were clearly 'hot niches', and while other countries showed property investment promise, I wasn't sure which would interest my potential ebook customers the most.

At this point I considered the smart thing to do would be some 'competition assessment' in each of these markets. The key factors I was interested in was how big the market was for people interested in investing in property in a particular country, and how much competition there was for those customers. In other words, I needed to know which ebooks would be popular and in demand, and whether there was actually a gap in the market for them that a new guide from me would fill.

Clearly, it would be no good writing a book on country X, only to discover the numbers would never add up as not enough people were interested in that market, or there was already a property investment guide written on it, or lots of information readily available online that would adversely affect my sales. This was a simple research exercise that I did on Google, looking at newspaper articles and news items about the countries on my 'Top 20' and looking up property investment information already in existence relating to those countries. I also used some free tools from Google – if you want to learn more about current trends visit *interpreneur.com/resources*

My research indicated that Slovakia and Turkey should be next on my list, and happily there was no shortage of countries to write about after that. Now my mind was really racing. I felt like I was sitting on a gold mine and I was very keen to start writing the next ebook and the next one. However, I also wanted to spend time on further research and looking ahead to grow the business, and how was I going to do that if I was spending approximately 60 hours writing each ebook?

I had heard people talk about 'outsourcing' websites where you could get people to do work for you, such as writing ebooks. So, logically,

I thought how I could outsource the compilation of the guides for me, which would free me up to expand my business faster. I could see how I could benefit from outsourcing enormously. If I outsourced the work of producing three books I could have at least three guides written in a few weeks instead of one, and I wouldn't have to do the research and writing myself. Using a quick Google search I found an outsourcing website, went over to the site and read the introduction to find out how the outsourcing of projects worked. *For a list of useful companies to outsource from see my resources page at interpreneur.com.*

To my surprise it was all fairly simple. All you needed to do was compile a description of what you required to be written and give some guidance on the size and style of the work. Then you placed this on the site and freelancers from around the world would bid for the project. Effectively the site works on what is known as a 'reverse auction' basis. The freelancers actually bid against each other, trying to undercut one another. So, for example, outsourcer A might bid $750, outsourcer B might then bid $700 and then outsourcer C might bid $650. So, by the time the auction closes the price is the minimum price that someone is prepared to complete the work for. I'd like to point out here that a low fee for a job does not mean you are exploiting someone. For example, the top ten highest monthly paying jobs in the Philippines earned workers approximately £380 - £630. So, this is not about trying to underpay – it is all about using the global market to mutual advantage, and the Internet makes this possible.

Anyhow, once all the bids are in you can look at the credentials of the bidders in terms of; their feedback scores from earlier completed tasks, the volume of work they have completed before and examples of their other work. Then you choose a winning bidder and 'award' the job to them. Once they have completed the project they hand over a first draft for your feedback. If you are happy at that stage you can just pay them, but more often than not you might ask for a bit of editing – perhaps more detail in some sections or removal of anything irrelevant. Once you are completely happy with the job you pay the outsourcer and your next project is all done.

I took the plunge, posted a job on the outsourcers' site and got my next guide written that way. The amazing thing about this process was the work was completed to a good standard for the equivalent of around £600. This meant that very often I could recover the outsourcer cost in the very first day of sales of a new product, so this system offered incredible leverage.

The power of this outsourcing meant my business started to grow FAST. I would give the outsourcer one of my earlier guides as a blueprint, and ask them to do the same thing for my next chosen property market. This is how my property guides on Slovakia, Turkey and then Slovenia, Florida and many more followed very quickly.

I learned a few fast lessons on outsourcing. Firstly, it is very important to look closely at the feedback scores and the volume of work delivered before by the outsourcer you want to hire. A couple of times I picked outsourcers who were too new or inexperienced and I was always disappointed. I also found that you have to take their proposed delivery dates with a pinch of salt. Outsourcers, it seems, are some of the unluckiest people on the planet. You will never cease to be amazed at how many of them fall over and break arms or fingers, how many of their relatives and pets get sick and require round-the-clock care, and how many develop major malfunctions with their computers or Internet which render them useless for weeks at a time. I am of course talking about the excuses outsourcers give you when they fail to deliver your project on time!

Now, from the outsourcer's perspective, I do have some sympathy. What you need to understand is that an outsourcer may bid on ten projects each week and reasonably expect to win one. If they happen to win four projects that week and have promised all four hirers they can deliver the work in a fortnight, they obviously have a problem. I learned a great solution to this that I call the 'ethical bribe'. Basically, if your winning bidder has bid, say, £300 for your project and has promised they can deliver in two weeks, I would offer to give them £350 (i.e. £50 ABOVE what they asked for) if/when they hit the agreed timescale. Then if they do overcommit themselves, guess whose project they complete first?

Go to Interpreneur.com/resources to get extra materials and free Internet Marketing training

The other major lesson I've learned from outsourcing surrounds copyright law. Technically, even if you pay someone to write an ebook for you and you pay them, they still own the intellectual copyright of that work. The way around this is to get something called a 'rights assignment form' signed by them before you complete payment. This then protects you as they have legally transferred all their Intellectual Rights in the product they have created over to you. You can find more about rights assignment forms in the resources page at *interpreneur.com.*

Plagiarism is another issue to consider again here. You can check copy is original by using the website *copyscape.com.*

After just three months I had made a lot of money, in fact more than I could ever have imagined. My dream car at the time was a Porsche, so I bought one that was just a couple of years old, and I actually paid cash. For some reason I had always wanted a bright yellow Porsche and so that's what I got. Not bad considering that just three months before I'd handed back the company car and downgraded to a 10-year-old Toyota Granvia. My new car's performance was just amazing and I loved the sound of the engine and its styling. I must admit it was not very practical, but it was certainly a lot of fun.

LESSON TIME! Simon Says:

If you have one good idea that makes you money on the Internet then there is another idea just waiting to be unleashed. Don't just sit back and count your cash – go and find your NEXT source of income!

If it ain't broke don't fix it – just rinse and repeat, again and again if you can.

Outsource. I simply could not have made the money I have without outsourcing tasks. Don't wait until you are at breaking point – use outsourcers to help you grow your business, don't wait until you're drowning in tasks and need them to rescue you.

Give outsourcers a bonus to ensure your job is top of their pile and they do it to the best of their ability.

Get outsourcers to transfer to you the Intellectual Rights of the work they have created for you.

Use *copyscape.com* to check for plagiarism.

CASE STUDY

Frankie Widdows

eyelashexcellence.com

After 10 years of chasing and fighting with suspects as a Police Dog Handler it was time for a career change! My passion in beauty therapy had nagged me for some time and in 2012, at the age of 30, I decided to make the jump from one career extreme to another. The biggest challenge for me was getting started and channelling my efforts and limited resources in the right direction. I had no idea where to find that direction and I felt a bit lost – after all I'd left a job that brought me a steady income of £2,000 net a month and had a handsome pension at the end of it.

I met Simon and researched how he and the *Internet Business School* could aid me and my individual circumstances, attending a course in 2013 and becoming one of Simon's business coaching students. With no business background, and even less knowledge on all things Internet, many around me viewed my trust and investment in Simon's services as a gamble. Happily, they were soon to be proved wrong, and their concerns unfounded.

The results were almost immediate, and my reputation and workload increased dramatically, which quickly lead me to becoming a trainer in the specific field of eyelash extensions. Simon's mentoring helped me to develop and guide my online business, and gave me direction to steer it towards where I wanted to be.

On top of delivering a range of courses in person I developed online courses, supported by DVDs, and then went on to delivering group courses. To my surprise and delight the demand for my work and courses rapidly expanded internationally, and I made the natural progression into product research and retail as my business grew, supplying products to the industry. This allowed me to employ technicians and support staff along the journey.

Now aged 34 and based in Kent I deliver a range of group training courses and online courses globally, which have paved the way for me to travel the world and network with others within my industry. I also host an online forum with worldwide members and run a busy online retail shop, 'Eyelash Excellence Ltd'.

The 'rags to riches' cliché is often used but is particularly relevant to my circumstances, as I started with only minimal funds and no direction yet have developed into a successful businesswoman with international recognition in my field and a portfolio of A-list clientele. My turnover is now a healthy £400k - £500k per year. The prospect of becoming a millionaire when I left the police was non-existent, and to achieve this within a few years is truly unbelievable for me. It has opened doors to a new world, allowed me to buy my favourite car and my dream house is on the way.

CHAPTER 6

Widening The Net

I now had a bright yellow Porsche and a thriving property investment guide business, but six months down the line a problem emerged that stopped this particular business growing any further. It was an inevitable stumbling block I suppose: I ran out of countries! Once I'd written a guide on all of the major countries UK investors were interested in buying in, my business naturally plateaued. It was time to take a step back and to have a think about what I had created.

Basically, I had found that people who were interested in a subject area - in my experience overseas property investment - were willing to pay around £10-£20 for detailed information about that subject. It didn't matter that almost all the information they were buying was readily available for free online if they looked hard enough, or found out where to look. What I was saving them was TIME. They didn't have to do their own research and gather all the relevant info together. I now knew very well indeed that it took me or an outsourcer anything from 50 to 100 hours to compile a guide, and so that's almost how long it would have taken the customers to research themselves. It made sense that they were prepared to pay me to put all the information in one place in front of them, nicely summarised, and all for less than £20. If you think about it, if it took somebody 50 hours to research the information for themselves and they valued their time, then they would be better off paying me £20 for the info – otherwise they would effectively be paying themselves just 40p an hour for doing the work themselves!

My brain was ticking over, processing these key facts and what they actually meant. Naturally I started to think about what other subjects, other than property investment, I could create an informational product around. If people were prepared to pay for research and information that was packed into a simple ebook, surely I just had to look for more topics people were sufficiently interested in to make other information-based ebooks worth buying?

A good friend of mine had mentioned that he had a cousin who was an Indian national yoga champion and had recently recorded a yoga training DVD. I did some research online and found that yoga was certainly a very popular subject on the Internet, so I thought why not try selling this product too?

I agreed to import a pallet load of DVDs from India and set about making a webpage to sell them from. Now, in hindsight, the cheaper way to do this sort of international deal would have been to import a single copy of the DVD and get hold of the artwork files, then duplicate the stock in the UK. As it was the consignment was intercepted by customs and I had to pay VAT on the retail value of the goods (about £500 before I'd even sold my first copy) just to get them into the country. I also had to drive to Charlton to collect the DVDs! All was not lost, because the product did sell well and I also learned some key lessons with this deal. I'll tell you more about this later, under the heading 'Post Problems' in the chapter on 'Growing Pains'.

On another day I was chatting to my old boss from BT, Geoff. We had kept in touch since I left the company and we were just having a general catch up when he mentioned in passing that his wife Anita had recently got into 'home staging', as a sideline to her regular job. I had to get him to explain exactly what that was, as initially I had no idea and had never even heard of the term, In a nutshell home staging is all about house makeovers; to 'stage' a home is to effectively make it look like a show home. After a bit of a discussion Geoff and I concluded that perhaps Anita could put together some informational products based on her knowledge of home staging, I could market them online and we could share the proceeds. We all agreed to give this a go.

With some research Anita and I identified two niches within the home staging market. The first was focused on people who wanted to sell their houses quickly and were looking for advice on how to secure a quick sale by using home staging techniques. The second niche involved providing business start-up training for people who wanted to create a home staging business themselves and become a home staging consultant like Anita.

Anita put two information products together to cater for these two different market niches, I created the websites to sell them and set about driving some traffic to them. The ebooks both sold well and within a few months Anita was earning enough from her 50% share of this endeavour to give up her separate day job and concentrate on this full-time. I'm very happy to say that since these early beginnings Anita has gone on to become one of the country's leading expert in home staging and has 'staged' show home properties for major housing developers, created kitchens and bathroom displays for a major chain of stores all over the country, and has featured in publications including *The Telegraph* and *House Beautiful.*

Another friend of mine was a grammar school teacher and one of the subjects he taught was the Theory of Knowledge. This is a mandatory subject in the International Baccalaureate (IB) syllabus (an alternative to A levels), but at the time there was very little in the way of established textbooks on the subject. My friend had handwritten notes that he had prepared himself and used when he taught the subject. Other teachers asked if they could use his notes as his students got great results, so I could immediately see that my friend had a ready-made product. Essentially his notes just needed typing up, and he would have an information product that we knew was in demand and people would be prepared to buy.

I helped him to get the notes typed up and encouraged my friend to also write some model answers to the examination questions, as I remembered from my own school days that these kind of practical study guides were the best. Of course students love model answers, but so do teachers as it saves them TIME preparing lessons. As I'd already learned, that's one of the key things about information products. Often the information in them is available for free elsewhere online, but what you are doing is putting quality, succinct information together in one place which is easy to consume. People are happy to pay a price for this and I figured the parents of grammar school students who were doing the IB would be very happy to buy a resource that would potentially help their child achieve the best grades.

When it came to creating the product my role was fairly minimal. I wrote the sales copy for the ebook and did the marketing, which basically meant sending customers searching for 'IB study guides', and words like this, to my website to make the sale. I did learn an interesting lesson on this one though. I found that because it was an educational textbook, a lot of people preferred to have a paper version, rather than just an ebook. I found this out through feedback to my website, when customers expressed surprise that it was not available as a hard copy. Of course, when I discovered this I addressed the issue, so as well as a download version I offered a paper version.

To my surprise I found that customers would pay almost TWICE as much (£32.95 versus £17.95) for the same information in hard copy. Furthermore the extra costs were only about £2 a unit, which meant much higher profits than for the ebook. Of course, this was my first foray into this type of publishing, but this didn't faze me. I learned from my previous experiences and used outsourcers to lay out the pages, design a logo and cover for the book, and so on. Whenever there was a new lesson to learn I embraced it rather than feeling overwhelmed. That was another lesson in itself: you can't be easily put off, and potential obstacles need to be seen as challenges to be overcome. Just ask yourself 'How can I do this?' because there is always a way.

I met another guy around this time who led me to create another information product. This man ran a cleaning business and he had an idea to write a manual on how you set up your own cleaning business. Now you might think this is not a really complicated subject, but actually there's a fair bit to it and the guide we created included things like; how to get clients, how much to charge, where to get cleaning materials wholesale. Plus he added advice on recruiting the right sort of staff, retaining them and legal things such as insurance and tax.

Believe it or not, there are cleaning business franchises that cost £20,000 or more. For that fee you get a business 'blueprint' as part of the package, which typically doesn't offer you much more in terms of information than the manual we compiled. However, buying a franchise also gets you a brand name of course, and possibly some leads from some national advertising, so we decided to come up with our own brand, and provided template documents such as contracts, invoices and so on. All this we decided to market for the sum of £77. Now although that may look expensive for an ebook, a brand name and a few template documents, when compared with a franchise costing £20,000 it was an absolute bargain!

I've been selling this product very successfully for ten years now and it's been a pretty 'evergreen' subject to sell information on, which is another lesson learned. Sometimes it's good to respond to a 'hot niche' but you should not overlook gaps in the market related to essential, perennial products and services.

This brings me on to an ebook I did for electricians. This one came about because the brother of the guitarist in the band was an electrician and I got talking to him about the essential information he needed to know in order to do his job safely. Through this conversation I discovered all about the '17th Edition Wiring Regulations', a set of new regulations that every electrician in the UK had to know and then pass an exam to demonstrate they could meet the required standard. The subject matter may have been as dull as ditch water but that didn't matter, because what we created was an up-to-date guide to passing exams for electricians, and of course there are tens of thousands of electricians working in the UK who had to know all this stuff. The ebook sold well and made us both a nice amount of money.

After a while I started running out of ideas for information products. I'd exhausted all the ideas from people I knew and so I needed new inspiration. I'd been to a few more business seminars and workshops by now, and I remembered a speaker at one of them had said that there are ideas and opportunities all around us every day. He said all you had to do was 'keep your head up and eyes open'. I thought about that phrase and started to look around everywhere I could for fresh ideas for yet more information products. I started paying more attention to the world around me, and made a particular effort to read newspapers. I actually found it quite invigorating to turn the pages of a newspaper and hunt for possible ideas every day. I had no idea what I might find – and that was very exciting.

LESSON TIME! Simon Says:

If you are selling information products, use your contacts and look close to home to find your information. What do you, your family and your friends and associates know about? Often people don't realise how valuable their knowledge is - and you could BOTH benefit from selling it in some way.

Don't import ready-made DVD products as you will have to pay tax on the sales value of all the combined units. Instead pay to bring a master copy to the UK, pay tax on that one item, and then duplicate in the UK!

Strike fair deals with the people you collaborate with – it's only right they have a 50% cut if they are providing all the content and you are simply packaging and selling it.

Keep your head up and your eyes open and never stop looking for new opportunities.

Hungry markets are the best, where your product is a necessity or a 'must have'.

A 'make money' or 'save money' product is usually a good bet, as people are more likely to be willing to make a purchase if they think they will gain or profit from it.

A 'nice to have' product is harder to sell but not impossible – sometimes if you catch the wave at the right time this kind of product can do very well.

CASE STUDY

Helen and Hugh Smith

studentspaceuk.com

My husband and I, both in our early sixties, attended a 3-day *Internet Business School* course in November 2015, after being impressed by Simon who had been speaking at another event we attended. We wanted to launch a new venture after long careers in education, and the 3-day course was just what we needed to explore the elements relating to running an online business.

We were originally teachers (music for my husband, computing for me), subsequently becoming teacher educators and university lecturers within the higher education sector.

In addition, we both had extensive educational experience covering a wide range of ages and stages, including teaching adults. Our business idea was to provide advice on techniques and approaches to achieving personal success in learning.

For our first venture we wrote a book called *The Students' Guide to Success at Almost Everything* (we attended a related writing/ publishing course from the *Internet Business School* on top of Simon's 3-day course) and we launched the book along with a companion website using the skills developed at Simon's course.

Our website is a forum for students to make requests, email for help, provide suggestions and is also a portal for continuing updates. It contains free stuff as well as a membership area. We are currently developing further books and have been approached to visit education and training establishments to provide workshops and seminars. Thanks to our backgrounds we have been able to access a large national and international network despite only being six months into our new venture.

At this stage in our lives we have not exclusively embarked on our business venture for lifestyle change reasons, although we do enjoy the freedom of working for ourselves from our home in Morecambe, and we appreciate the time that we invest and spend together on projects and business developments.

The course offered by the *Internet Business School* was just what we had been looking for. There was headroom for thinking and to question and challenge our thoughts and plans. It confirmed to us that we both had valuable skill sets, expertise and ideas worth developing into a new business, and that there is life after working full-time for an employer. Above all, we seemed to have 'stuff' in our heads that others wanted which was a completely different way of looking at things.

Life is extremely interesting and we are very glad to have embarked on this exciting new business venture at a stage in life when most people are thinking of retiring. We would not have been motivated to grasp the opportunity without attending Simon's course (including the related writing/publishing course), and if our first six months are anything to go by, we are hopeful to have continued success (and increasing profits) in the years to come.

CHAPTER 7

A Universe Of Ideas

I learned that newspapers have ideas for businesses in them EVERY day and I learned how to read the papers in the best way to find ideas. Here's what I found particularly useful:

- **Stories that are about NEW trends, fads and crazes.** For example, when electric cars first started to appear, people would obviously be looking for information on their efficiency, performance and cost-effectiveness, so was it worth writing a guide? If someone were going to spend thousands on a car they would probably be happy to spend £20 on a guide to help them make the right choice.

- **Financial pages**. These tell you which companies are doing well and not so well. Guess what that means? It spells out for you what are hot profitable markets and which things are in decline.

- **Adverts**. It makes sense that businesses that regularly take out large adverts must be doing well. Again, this is an environmental signal of what is a great market to be in right now.

It was through reading the *Daily Mail* one day that I stumbled on an unlikely business opportunity. I saw an advert selling 'moon plots'. Yes, you've read that correctly! A man in Cornwall was actually selling plots of land on the moon. I Googled 'who owns the moon?' and discovered that in the 60s all the major countries in the world signed a treaty agreeing that no country was allowed to stake a claim on the moon. However, it turned out that an American businessman had cottoned on to the fact the agreement was solely about countries and not individuals, and so he had filed a claim on the moon in his own name. He then carved it up into one-acre plots which he sold as novelty gifts, a bit like the way you can 'buy' a star in the sky as a present.

The guy in Cornwall had purchased the rights to selling plots in the UK so I called him and asked if he would sell me some wholesale moon. My thinking was that I could then sell it over the Internet rather than through adverts in national newspapers – he didn't have a website - and that way I could make a tidy profit. He was selling plots to the public for £29.95 each but agreed to sell me 100 plots at the wholesale price of £9 an acre. I then created a website from which to sell the plots to British customers.

Crucially, I realised nobody was going to search for 'moon plots for sale' on the Internet, but I figured that what they would search for was 'unusual birthday gift'. It wasn't rocket science! I simply applied skills I had developed around SEO or search engine optimisation, as I've touched on before, to make sure that I got my website to the top of Google for anyone searching for that phrase.

Happily, I sold out in two weeks, making a profit of more than £20 a time, which banked me over £2,000 for very little effort and the cost of creating a website, which was less than £3 to register a domain name. I then called the Cornish businessman and asked if I could order another 500 plots for an even better wholesale price of £7. He agreed, and to my delight he then came out with the unlikely and very unexpected line: 'Did you know I've also got Jupiter and Mars, if you're interested?'

Eventually this business ran its course after my supplier in Cornwall started to sell wholesale moon to other traders who subsequently undercut the price on a plot of land to £22.95 and then less and less. This of course undermined my supplier's business, so he ultimately stopped selling wholesale plots of land and just created his own website to sell to UK customers.

I had absolutely no regrets. I'd made a profit and learned a lesson: in hindsight I perhaps could have negotiated a 12-month minimum price on the wholesale rights in return for an exclusive arrangement. It didn't matter, I was learning all the time, and I was open to new challenges. If a crazy idea like that could turn me a profit, then the World Wide Web really was my oyster.

After my moon adventure I spotted a story in the press that got a lot of people talking. A squatter had successfully taken legal possession of a one million pound property in Hampstead, North London after proving that he had maintained it and lived in the abandoned house for more than 10 years. 'I wonder if there are other properties like that, ones that I could take over?' was the question on a lot of minds. 'If so, what are the rules, and how do you go about it?'

I had another question. 'If so many people are interested in this story, why don't I create an information product about it?'

I Googled the Land Registration Act 2002 and, in a nutshell, I rewrote the Act in layman's terms and created a plain English guide explaining how to legally claim free property, land and building plots using what are known as 'adverse possession laws'. It sold like hot cakes for a while (more about this later!), even though the information I was selling was all readily available from the Land Registry, if you could be bothered to plough through the legalese and make sense of it.

Another information product that grew from a newspaper article was a guide on how to become a plumber. The news story I read this time told how a City trader had jacked in his job and was retraining as a plumber, because at the time plumbers were in short supply and therefore high demand, the money plumbers were earning was really good – enough to rival a City trader's earnings. As with the squatter's story, people were asking themselves how they could replicate the success of the person in the news story. What did it take to become a plumber? How did you go about it?

I could see there was definitely a gap in the market and so I created an ebook called *How to Become a Plumber.* This was so popular that I eventually expanded into providing a DVD and training course on the same subject, but I'll explain more about courses later. Suffice to say at this point in time I have generated more than £200,000 from my plumbing books and courses, and I have replicated the success with plastering and bricklaying – trades that are always going to be in demand. All this and I've never even changed a tap washer in my life!

Another product that came from a news story I spotted was an ebook guide telling you all you needed to know about bonsai trees. I read that bonsais were very popular at the time and sales were rising, so I bought the resale rights to a guide that had already been written. I did this by Googling 'resale rights Bonsai Trees' and then selling the book online using my tried and tested methods.

Like I say, it's not rocket science. For the price of a newspaper you have a wealth of inspiration at your fingertips. Keep your eyes and ears open all the time, and read as much as you can, every day. Knowledge is never wasted, and it can prove to be very profitable.

LESSON TIME! Simon Says:

When reading newspapers pay particular attention to stories about new trends, fads and crazes, keep an eye on the financial pages to see which companies are performing well and check out the adverts as they tell you which markets are performing well.

Some of the craziest ideas and most imaginative can turn a profit – never be too afraid to give seemingly wacky or non-mainstream ideas a try. Nobody will laugh at you when they realise how much money you've made!

If you hit on a good resale product, think about negotiating an exclusive agreement to keep copycats at bay.

CASE STUDY

Tom Druitt

thebiglemon.com

I launched the Big Lemon in 2007, realising the dream of setting up an alternative local bus service in Brighton, where I live. Crucially, I wanted it to be affordable, environmentally sustainable and a pleasure for passengers to use. Our buses and coaches run on waste cooking oil that we collect from restaurants, process and clean up so it can be used as fuel. Passengers love having a green transport alternative – the carbon footprint from cooking oil compared with diesel is 95% lower - and we pride ourselves on offering a friendly service.

The business grew quite quickly at the start but I came across some teething problems and growing pains and things went a bit wobbly for a while. I wanted to cut costs and, after realising we were spending a lot on our website, I decided to learn how to do my own website and promotion on the Internet. I didn't know a thing about web design or Internet marketing - and that's how I came to do a course at the *Internet Business School*.

Thanks to Simon I learned to design my own website, do my own Internet marketing, how to get the best out of YouTube and social media plus, crucially, how to get Big Lemon on the first page of Google. I saw results straightaway and found it was much more effective and less costly and stressful than it had been when we hired web designers. After a year of doing Simon's course the business grew from having three vehicles to seven, and now we have eight buses and three coaches. The huge jump has been down to the increased traffic to the website. Brand awareness improved dramatically and bookings shot up once the new website was up and running.

Since I started working with Simon our business has grown by 50% and since last October our turnover has increased by £250k. For a relatively small investment in Simon's course it's been massively worth it for me, and the results are impressive.

When I first met Simon he said if I provided the passion, energy and drive for my business he would give me the know-how, knowledge and tools to make it work. Simon focused very much on providing a practical toolkit for turning ideas into reality, getting the word out there and getting the numbers right, but that is not all. In guiding me through the process he gave me more energy and passion for my business – so I have to disagree with his original pledge!

I now have a platinum membership to the *Internet Business School*, as I want to keep my skills fresh and up to date. I also enjoy the social side of meeting other students. They've all got interesting businesses, we help each other out and there's an active Facebook group for support too.

Simon's guidance has been invaluable. In September 2016 The Big Lemon scooped three awards at the Brighton & Hove Business Awards: the Green Business award, Best Place to Work and Business of the Year. It really is a dream come true.

CHAPTER 8

Reviewing The Situation

A few of my former colleagues from BT had decided to take their redundancy money and invest it in a franchise, with varying degrees of success. I listened to some of their stories – and especially the ones that hadn't worked out - and wondered why they hadn't been able to find out more about the likely success of their chosen franchise business before they parted with their precious redundancy pay-outs.

It didn't make sense to me that if you were going to buy a kettle or a toaster for £20 or £30 you could look up consumer reviews in the likes of *Which?* Magazine to help you make an informed choice, but if you were parting with tens of thousands of pounds and trying to decide which was the best franchise or business opportunity to invest in then you had virtually nowhere to turn to get the inside track.

I came up with a way of solving this problem, and my idea was to create a website called *Business Opportunity Review (business-opportunity-review.co.uk)* which would provide reviews of franchises and other business opportunities. It would essentially be a review site, and my thoughts were that my customers would pay a subscription fee to be a 'member' and read the reviews on the site, and that is how I would make my money.

I figured that if people were prepared to buy a subscription to something like *Which?* Magazine for consumer goods then they would certainly part with a membership fee to access my website. With business opportunity schemes costing hundreds to thousands of pounds, and franchises costing as much as £25,000 or more, a small monthly membership fee would be a very small price to pay for some 'due diligence' and reassurance they had done their homework before making a substantial investment.

It sounded like a good plan, but when I launched the site I soon found there were some core issues that needed ironing out. The first challenge I had to overcome was the classic 'chicken and egg' one. When the site was new there were only seven reviews posted, which were schemes that some friends of mine had tried and could write an honest, informative review on. I originally envisaged that members who joined the site would not only read the reviews already posted, but they would be encouraged to contribute their own reviews, hence the site would grow and improve all the time. However, not surprisingly, in the early days nobody would pay a membership fee to read just seven reviews and so I needed to have a re-think.

The new idea I came up with was to offer membership for free for a limited time in exchange for sending a review in of a business opportunity or franchise. This worked to great effect and the site had 100 reviews within a week and over 500 in the first month. At this point a nominal fee of £4.95 per month was introduced and members started joining at the rate of 20 plus new members per day. I'm happy to say that since its launch over 11,000 people have joined the site, membership revenues have exceeded £1 million and the site is still performing well a decade on – all from a simple idea and a bit of time and effort!

Business Opportunity Review has had several enhancements during its lifetime and this has been key to keeping members on board. One great tip I learned from this venture is to ask the customer precisely what they want. Lots of members wanted to be able to see the average score of all reviews for a given type of business, and a league table of the top-scoring opportunities, so they could quickly see which looked to be the best schemes. Of course, I gave them what they asked for.

One of the ways the site encourages members to send in reviews is by holding prize draws for contributors from time to time. In addition, content has been donated by relevant experts in the field, such as from a solicitor who gave advice from a legal perspective on how to get money back when scammed and so on. This is of course a free plug for their business, so it's a win-win deal.

Over time I realised I was building up a valuable mailing list of members, as not only did I have the thousands of paying members, but tens of thousands of people who had signed up for the site's newsletter. To date, this total number has reached 76,000. I could see that I had basically two lots of 'customers' – the paying members and the non-paying 'interested parties' – and at this point I decided to introduce a two-tier membership instead of the nominal monthly fee. The fact there were other competing sites emerging when I made this decision was also a factor here. I needed to stay competitive, and to do this I had to keep growing the number of reviews posted. With this in mind I offered a free basic membership where you could see a limited number of reviews, as this would encourage people to post their own reviews, plus I brought in what I now called the 'Gold' membership at £4.95 per month, which gave you access to all the reviews and average scores and brought the money in. In addition, an annual fee of £57 was offered which gave a discount when compared with the monthly fees, so hopefully everybody was happy.

In terms of retention of members, several strategies have been introduced over time. Firstly, bonus gifts that exceed the cost of membership are given out on a regular basis, and these are normally digital products that don't incur delivery costs. Introducing and encouraging an active forum on the site has been another way of keeping members on board. There's also ongoing legal advice and free website hosting offered to paying members.

Another way of 'monetising' the site over the years has been by placing adverts within the content of the site. These have included Google ads, which are   selected and run by Google. Revenue from the ads is shared, generating a revenue share that has exceeded $1,000 per month.

You might be thinking at this point that I sailed through the early years of being an Interpreneur without any hassles, and that everything I touched turned to gold. It's true that *Business Opportunity Review* was yet another great business success for me, but it did also bring its problems – in fact it generated the biggest problem I'd encountered since starting out on my own.

One particular business opportunity on the site had had a few reviews submitted from the public, several of which weren't very complimentary and called into question the reliability of the business scheme. The seller of this particular business opportunity took offence at the negative reviews and wrote to me asking me to remove them from the site. As the whole point of the site was to provide a place where the public could share their honest and true experiences I didn't really want to remove the negative reviews. I told the company that I was not going to remove them as we lived in a land of 'free speech'. I added that the comments from reviewers reflected their own genuine experience and as such they were valid and therefore should be allowed to be reported.

The company did not accept this, appointed solicitors and started a legal spat. I consulted my own solicitor to see exactly what the legal position was and was informed that as the website owner I was responsible for the accuracy of anything reported on my site. Furthermore, if this company wanted to sue me they could, despite the fact their complaint related to a review that was submitted from a third party. If the complainant successfully sued me I would have to counter sue the review submitter for any of my own costs and damages. On top of this, if I had means to pay the company suing me (I did) then I'd have to pay, but if the original author of the review this related to didn't have any money and I counter-sued them to reclaim my losses, I could end up out of pocket! Even worse, the complaining company was now alleging 'defamation' against me. I was told that defamation cases can only be heard in a High Court, which meant my minimum legal bill to fight this would be around £25,000. If I won I might only expect to get two-thirds of the costs back so I would still be out of pocket. That's not very fair, is it? NO, IT IS NOT!

Unfortunately in this case I decided the sensible thing to do would be to remove the offending reviews to get the other company to stand down. The learning point here is that sometimes being 'right' isn't always enough, and sometimes you have to compromise on your ideals in business. So, the big lesson here is to please remember you are legally responsible for all your own websites and everything on them. Always make sure you are crystal clear about all information you quote and report, and it is a good idea to protect yourself with legal protection insurance. If an issue arises, take expert legal advice. A good tip is to join the Federation of Small Businesses, because you get business insurance and a legal helpline included for free that may come in useful.

In time, other problems emerged too in relation to the review site. Owners of a few business schemes realised that a site like *Business Opportunity Review* was a great way of finding their target audience. Of course, I had the email list of all these potential 'customers' and the owners of the business schemes didn't, so what did they do? Several of them set up their own review sites in competition. Some were better than others and some were just a front for business owners to promote the business opportunities they were selling. Anyhow, the point of all this is that it changed my business. With so much competition, and so many sites offering free membership, I had to rethink what I was doing. In the end, my site became a free service, because why would anybody pay to read reviews on my site when they could access reviews for free on other sites? It didn't matter that I had built up a great database of genuine and extremely useful reviews. When you're selling something the customer thinks they can get for free, your business has to change.

The way I changed was this; I eventually decided to use the site as a 'lead generator' for other businesses. I did this by using it as a 'data capture' site. The details members gave me via their free memberships told me what they were interested in and this information was valuable to me. It's the same model Facebook uses – you don't pay to join Facebook, but your 'free membership' gives Facebook a lot of information it can use in other areas of business.

None of this happened overnight, of course. Oh no! First I went through a few more growing pains, all the time learning from my mistakes and of course keeping my entrepreneurial eyes and ears wide open, looking and listening for ways to grow my businesses and stay one step ahead of the curve.

Before I finish this chapter I'll give you another good example of how keeping your eyes and ears open is key to making money. When I was working from home I decided to install air-conditioning around house. I often joke that having a nice air-conditioned building to work in is the only thing I missed from BT – and that's not too far from the truth!

I Googled air-conditioning units and was frustrated to find that every company I came across that was selling air-con units wanted to send someone to my house to do a site survey before I could make a purchase. I was too impatient for this and wanted a simple off-the-peg system that I could order today and bolt to my wall tomorrow.

They say necessity is the mother of invention, and in this case it certainly was.

I could see there was a gap in the market here, so I called around the suppliers and suggested a deal. It went like this. If I could bring them orders with zero cost or marketing, would they give me a commission on the sale? I knew they must have advertising costs and sales staff costs to generate sales, so I figured they should be happy to give me that percentage if I gave them an order with none of those overheads.

I got three separate suppliers to agree to this and then created the online store by building a website that was basically just copied from the suppliers' own sites, with one crucial difference. My site had a 'Buy Now' button added. Each time I made a sale the customer paid me direct and then I sent 80% of the payment to the supplier. I never even touched the products as they went direct from the manufacturer to the customer. It worked very well and made me a tidy profit – after all, on a fairly typical £2,000 order I was getting £400.

Unfortunately, something changed that I had no control over – sales dropped when the temperature cooled at the end of the summer! So what did I do next? I started selling heating units – what else? I called this new business 'Total Heat Control'. Even today it still gives me a warm glow when I think about how simple it was to set this up!

LESSON TIME! Simon Says:

Don't be afraid to tinker with your initial business plan if it doesn't deliver as you expected.

If you hit a hurdle, look at all possible ways you can overcome it. It might be that you offer something for free for a limited time to get your business off the ground.

DON'T flog a dead horse though. Free offers should be for a limited period and you need to make sure they are not costing you anything – it's smart to give away access to a membership website or information that is already created, but not so clever to offer free physical goods and services, particularly those that need shipping!

Consider placing adverts within the content of your site – it can provide a great additional source of income.

Know the law. YOU as the website owner are responsible for the accuracy of everything on your site.

Know when to admit defeat. Sometimes it's better to walk away from a legal battle, even when you know you are right. Be the bigger person and chalk it up to experience.

Join the Federation of Small Businesses and benefit from free business insurance.

Think about your mailing list and the data you have amassed about your customers. Could you use this to grow your business or expand in other areas?

If you have trouble buying something online or sourcing a product you think other people are searching for too, congratulations! You've discovered a gap in the market – go and fill it!

CASE STUDY

Bill Goldie

strickland-protocol.com

When one of my children, Leanne, was diagnosed with Osgood Schlatter disease at the age of 12 I struggled to find information on how to help her. The condition causes a painful lump below the kneecap in children and adolescents experiencing a growth spurt in puberty, and it often affects children who participate in sport for more than 12 hours per week, as Leanne did.

After doing my own research I came across an experienced international Chartered Physiotherapist called Jenny Strickland. She developed 'The Strickland Protocol' which is the only scientifically proven cure in the world for Osgood Schlatters. It's easy to follow and only takes a few minutes each day, so you can imagine how delighted I was to finally have a cure for my daughter.

I wanted to share this information and so I asked Jenny to put together a treatment manual to help other kids and their parents. That is where Simon came in. I didn't know how to create and market a book so, at the age of 46, I went on one of his 2-day courses and followed up with several book-writing courses. That was in 2007, and in the 10 years since then I have sold more than £200,000 worth of treatment manuals in ebook and paperback form. Most importantly, we have helped over 5,000 parents who prior to hearing about our treatment had no idea how to get their kids pain free and back to sport.

Over the past ten years I have continued to be mentored by Simon and his team and I've done several refresher courses on book publishing. Whenever I have an issue or something new comes up Simon is very good at getting information to me, so I continue to benefit from his training today. I've done all the work on the manual from my home in Hextable, Kent, working just a few hours per week, as I also have my own business, helping companies buy industrial parts from China.

I'd certainly recommend Simon's courses. Without him I definitely would not have achieved such success, and many more parents and kids would be struggling with Osgood Schlatters like my family was back in the early 2000s. Thank you Simon.

CHAPTER 9

Growing Pains

Let me tell you about a few of the other growing pains I went through along the way, and how I dealt with them. This is an important chapter, because as well as learning from my successes, I learned from every one of my mistakes. So, my message is this. Don't expect everything to be plain sailing, but just be grateful that problems are very rarely as bad as they could have been. Most importantly, keep in mind that you ALWAYS learn from problems.

I'm not too proud to talk you through a long and varied list of 'glitches' I've encountered over the years, so here goes:

Post problems

Remember that I was selling the yoga DVDs I imported from India? This went well, despite the initial hitch with my first consignment being intercepted by customs, and of course I was also selling several other information-based DVDs and CDs, such as my info products on plumbing and plastering. It was all going very well as sales were good, but I soon hit a very practical problem that I hadn't foreseen.

My house was in a small close, and my nearest postbox at the end of the close was one of those little rectangular boxes attached to a post and designed to hold the odd birthday card and letter. However, as I started selling my CDs and DVDs I was posting them in padded 'Jiffy' bags. Depending what other people in the neighbourhood had posted, I could normally get about 12 discs in the little postbox before it was full. Whenever that happened I'd have to drive to the nearest postbox in the next village. Unfortunately, that postbox was also one of those small ones, so once I exceeded about 24 discs a day I'd have to drive to the NEXT village! In the end I'd be dropping at three or four postboxes a day. The nearest town with a full-size postbox was about eight miles away, so even though it was a nuisance to have to tour the local postboxes it was quicker than driving to the town, and this rigmarole became a daily ritual at around 3 p.m. each afternoon.

One day, when I was running a bit late, I got to postbox number 3 and was just putting the last of my packages in when the postman pulled up in his red van to empty the postbox. He jumped out of his van, staring at me and pointing, and said quite aggressively, 'It's YOU!' I thought this was a strange way to greet someone who was a very good customer of his employer, the Royal Mail, but anyway I said to him, 'Yes, if you mean I'm the person posting rather a lot of padded envelopes recently then, yes, it's me!' The postman then went on to tell me that I had been causing a lot of problems I was blissfully unaware of.

Apparently the local sorting office had been getting lots of calls from people trying to post letters between 3 p.m. and the collection around 5 p.m., who had turned up and found the postboxes were stuffed full. People had apparently started thinking the Royal Mail simply wasn't emptying the boxes every day, as they should. To my horror the postman asked me if I realised that old age pensioners, for example, had been trying to post birthday cards to their grandchildren. When they found their local postbox full they had taken a bus to the next village only to find that was full up too. I had no idea and I felt terrible!

The postman explained that as I was clearly posting a large amount of letters every day the Royal Mail would come and collect from my house. They would do this for free, given the volume of mail I was generating and therefore the amount of money I was spending with the Royal Mail. Why hadn't I thought of asking if that were possible? Anyhow, that's what I did from then on. In the end it was an easy solution, but I still feel bad about the inconvenience I had unknowingly put all those people through.

I guess the lesson here is that if you encounter a problem, don't just clutch at the nearest solution. Think it through and don't be afraid to ask questions, and you will probably be surprised at the answer and at what help is available to you. I was not doing anything wrong in having a large stash of parcels to post every day, and it would have been a lot easier if I'd picked up the phone in the beginning, been upfront and asked the simple question of the Royal Mail: 'What's the best way for me to post my parcels?' Simple!

Go to Interpreneur.com/resources to get extra materials and free Internet Marketing training

Staff shortfalls

It quickly became a full-time job just making, packing and posting in excess of 100 discs a day, and as the business went on I had to take on some administration staff to help with all the production and packing up of the various CDs and DVDs.

The interview process was quite quick and easy. I figured that as the job simply involved burning the relevant discs each day and posting them out to the customer who had ordered them it wasn't really too hard a task. Some of the candidates who came for the jobs even had a degree and were just looking to earn some extra cash, and I had absolutely no concerns they could do this simple job without a hitch. Unbelievably, that's where I was wrong!

I started getting complaints from people who had ordered a DVD on plastering, for example, and received the right box but with a DVD on plumbing inside. Close, but it was not what they wanted! Even worse, some people were receiving a really nice EMPTY box! Often this resulted in a refund request as the customer had understandably lost confidence in us. Worse still was a 'chargeback' from the credit card company, which incurred not only a refund but also a £15 charge from them for processing the transaction. I couldn't understand how the people I'd taken on to help me were failing on such a basic task, but to be fair I guess with the sheer volume of discs going out the door, human error kicked in. With more than 100 discs a day to deal with you only needed a 1% error rate to create problems every day.

The solution to this was ultimately very simple, and it's something common to many 'fulfilment' businesses that have a product to deliver. The answer was to put in place a process whereby another person checked the order before it finally went out. So, one person would prepare the orders and pack them but not seal the packages. Another person would then just double-check the right disc was in the correct package (and that no more than was ordered was in the package, which turned out to be an occasional problem that of course no one actually complained about!) The packing problem was solved, at last.

Go to Interpreneur.com/resources to get extra materials and free Internet Marketing training

Green-eyed monsters

I'm afraid that one of the other problems you're likely to encounter when you have a successful business is that ugly side of human nature - JEALOUSY! I was running this DVD and CD business, as well as my other Internet-based enterprises like *Business Opportunity Review,* literally out of my spare room. As my business had grown and I'd taken on a couple of people to assist me, as I've just explained, they were coming to work from my house each day. Normally these people would park on the driveway of the three-bed detached house I was now living in, which had room for three or four cars, but occasionally one of them would park on the road. The close I lived in was small, with about ten houses, and there was always plenty of room to park on the street without stealing anyone's space. However, that did not mean keeping the neighbours happy wasn't an issue I didn't have to deal with.

I'd bought myself a brand new Land Rover Discovery by now as I was doing so well (the Porsche was long gone – I only had it for a year before I realised how impractical it was!). One day I was horrified to see that some unkind person had decided to run a key down the entire length of my shiny new Discovery. As I lived on a small no-through road, nobody but the neighbours and their visitors and delivery people had any cause to enter the close. I could only assume that somebody who was jealous of my new car had decided to give in to the green-eyed monster and do this damage as a way of getting to me. Sad, but I'm afraid true.

Then, on another day, I got a knock on the door and was greeted by three officials from the local council. They informed me it had been brought to their attention, by a neighbour's complaint, that I was running a business from my house without the appropriate permissions, and they wanted to inspect the premises. They came in and had a look round; I invited them in willingly, as I really had no idea about the 'appropriate permissions' they were talking about. I had one room with five desks in it, with two people working at them, plus disc duplicating machines on the other three desks. The council officials informed me that I did not have planning permission to run a business from home and I would need it for this 'material change of use', which was unlikely to be granted as I was in a residential area.

'So what can I do?' I asked, immediately thinking there had to be some way round this.

The reply sounded expensive and time-consuming: I was told I should immediately move the business into proper offices with a 'B1 classification' for business use. Thanks, nosy neighbour! It seemed that someone's sour grapes about me growing a successful business from home and taking on staff who occasionally had to park on the street near a neighbour's house was forcing me to find a new office location for my business. Cheers!

Jealousy seems to be a problem you can't escape and can raise its ugly head at any time, often when you least expect it. For instance, many years later, when I had moved to a much bigger property, my neighbours asked me to pay £5,000 in order for my builders to step foot on their land to access a roof they were replacing. The neighbours' reasoning was the building being reroofed was part of a commercial venture and 'you can afford to pay'. Very neighbourly!

So, be warned. As you become successful some people will inevitably resent that success no matter how hard you worked for it or how you choose to spend your money and live your life. My advice is to just be the better person. I believe, generally, that what goes around comes around, so don't let it bring you down and don't be pulled down to their level. You are too busy being an even more successful Interpreneur to become involved in bitter, energy-sapping spats.

Knock-off nuisances

One of the advantages of an information publishing business is the barriers to entry are almost non-existent. With no start-up capital you can have a good idea, turn it into an information product, set up a website and start driving traffic to it very quickly. Whilst this is great, it also means that your competitors can launch copycat products just as easily – so here are a few insights and tips surrounding the problem of knock-offs and competition.

As I mentioned earlier, one of the information products I created was a guide on claiming abandoned land and property, using adverse possession laws as part of the Land Registration Act 2002. I foolishly shared the story of this book when I was asked to speak at a seminar. I freely gave out details of how I wrote the book, how I marketed it and how many I was selling. Perhaps it's hardly surprising that within weeks I had competitors!

One particular person didn't even bother to write their own version but was just selling a complete copy of my book. Another undercut my £29.95 price by a couple of pounds to £27.95. I cut mine to £24.95, they cut theirs to £22.95, then they went down to £19.95 – and this went on until the price we were charging was almost £5 and the margin was so low it was barely worth selling. Today you can find this information on eBay for less than £1. So, the lesson here is that a market that was really profitable at £29.95 was eroded to a commodity product for a few pounds over the course of a few months, simply because I didn't keep my mouth shut, and I had too much faith in others not to blatantly copy off my idea.

How can you reduce the risk of copycats undermining your business? Well, if you can come up with a unique title or brand for your product, this is certainly a good start. You can register a trademark for a few hundred pounds and this gives you an amount of protection in law against people ripping off your name. Your content is protected automatically under copyright law, so if someone does a word for word copy you can litigate against him or her. BUT always remember that anyone can get an outsourcer or freelancer to write an original book on any subject for around $1,000, so do be very be careful!

If you build your business right and have a 'sales funnel' behind your front end product, then you should be in a position where you can afford to GIVE AWAY your front end product and still make a great income from the back end. This of course gives you protection if your front end product is copied. However, it's always good to monetize the front end too if at all possible. If you're scratching your head at this point, let me elaborate.

A sales funnel, quite simply, is the buying process a seller leads a customer through. This can be as simple as making the customer aware of your product, getting them interested in it and then securing the sale and perhaps then offering the customer the chance to buy additional items or to replace the product after a certain amount of time.

A good example of this is my *Internet Business School,* where I offer a range of introductory courses on Internet marketing topics, but also offer an accredited diploma in Internet marketing and complete business mentoring services for customers who want more - I'll go into further detail about this later.

Data dramas

Another problem I've had to deal with is losing data. This happened when my laptop crashed with a hard disk failure; the drive completely died and all data on it was lost. The original files relating to several of the products and websites I had created were lost, which meant I needed to recreate the content from scratch. This cost me hundreds of hours of work. Then I moved to having data backed up to an external drive, but I found that without automatic backup software remembering to run the backup every day it didn't happen, as I often forgot. I also learned that some software lets you schedule automatic backups, but these only work when your computer is turned on at the specific time and the external drive is connected.

Now I use *Dropbox.com* as a great way to backup all my data and seamlessly share it between all my computers. You don't even have to think about it, which works for me. Every time you save a document Dropbox is automatically backing it up into the Cloud within seconds, provided you are online. If you aren't online it will do this next time you are connected to the Internet.

LESSON TIME! Simon Says:

If you have a problem don't just clutch at the nearest solution. Think about the best way to solve it and don't be afraid to ask questions. You will probably be surprised at the answer and at what help is available to you.

Just because YOU think it's easy don't assume that your **staff** – however qualified or educated they are - will find it easy too. What I do now is give staff a practical test at interview. They have to answer a number of questions and complete tasks that relate to the sort of things they need to do in the job. It makes sense really, doesn't it?

When it comes to other people's **jealousy** there isn't much you can do about this, but I'd advise you not to be too 'flash' with your success. The manifestation of jealousy can be pretty nasty, so do your best to limit the risk of it happening to you.

If you are '**working from home**' that is fine, but if you start recruiting other people to work for you and have them coming to work in your house that can make a material 'change of use'. I'd suggest at the point where you take on your first employee you should also look to take on an external office or business premises - especially if you have neighbours twitching behind their net curtains!

Consider having a **trademarked** brand that you use to differentiate your products, and to offer a barrier to entry for competitors, and don't tell anyone else what your Internet business does or how successful it is.

Don't build your business around one product, also always prepare for a market to be potentially killed by rogue **competition** overnight. Operate in different markets and have a 'funnel' so you have a range of 'back end' products that are where the real money is made.

Go to Interpreneur.com/resources to get extra materials and free Internet Marketing training

Make sure you **back up** everything in your business, both locally on another machine or external hard disk, and externally in the Cloud (using something like *Dropbox.com*), just in case the worst happens and your house burns down or a jumbo jet lands on it.

CASE STUDY

Stephen Conway

portraitartist.co.uk and stonehengecottages.com

I wasn't sure how much I would learn from Simon's courses but I had a little voice inside my head nagging me to attend and so I did, in 2011. It was a very wise decision.

I had just started two new businesses at the age of 45 - an online art gallery representing a number of portrait artists, plus I had three upmarket holiday apartments, called Stonehenge Cottages, to let.

As these were completely new businesses to me I was on a very steep learning curve and may have made some fundamental mistakes had I not met Simon and his team.

One of the errors of my thinking for the holiday business was that I could keep a simple diary for bookings and manage the whole process myself. After a chat with Simon he made me aware of the need for a centralised online booking system that was already plugged into the main channel partners within the holiday industry, like *Booking.com*, *LateRooms.com*, *Expedia* etc. I researched the market and found a fantastic online booking system that was not only inexpensive but also fitted perfectly for my business.

That one single tip resulted in my new business growing from a standing start to a turnover of more than £200,000 in under 18 months. We now have 98% occupancy and are the highest rated accommodation out of 60 other hotels on *booking.com* in our local area. We have also won multiple awards and have many customers repeat booking with us each year.

On my portrait business, a simple conversation with one of

Simon's coaches resulted in her doing a small amount of SEO work to get my site ranked higher on Google. Within a few hours of the change my listing went from the bottom of page one to second place, which not only shocked me, but also meant this business now creates over £150,000 of revenue each year, with a high profit margin.

Needless to say I am very glad I attended *Internet Business School.* Simon and his team have given me advice that has helped generate more business that I could have ever hoped for.

CHAPTER 10

What Exactly
Do You Do, Simon?

When you're an Interpreneur it's often hard to explain exactly what you do. In the early days friends and family would be forever asking what I was doing. I would tell them I had set myself up as an 'Internet marketer' or an 'information publisher'. If pressed I'd tell them about some of the books I'd written on different subjects, but I could tell they found it hard to equate what I was saying about an ebook on some dull electrical wiring regulations, say, and how my fortunes had clearly taken such a sharp upwards turn. Not only did I buy the yellow Porsche just a few months after leaving BT, but I also started making home improvements and applied for planning permission to put a large extension on my house. People were asking questions and I'm not surprised!

One good friend, Rick, who's the drummer in my band, seemed really interested in what I was doing and pressed for more and more information on how I created products, how I sold them, how I made webpages and so on. After a while I suggested he come over for a half-day so I could show him how it all worked.

So, Rick and I arranged to meet up one afternoon. I showed him how to create an ebook, how to design a simple webpage using a free template, and how to generate traffic to the site from Google, instantly. I explained the process really wasn't that hard, and I found myself telling him what I'd learned for myself, which is that you only need three things:

1 Something to sell

2 Somewhere to sell from (your website)

3 Someone to sell to (traffic)

For Step One we discussed some ideas and concluded that, as Rick was currently working for the Kent Fire and Rescue Service and had some knowledge of the recruitment process, then the ideal thing for him to sell would be an ebook on how to get a job in the fire service. Rick told me the jobs were quite sought after, particularly by ex-military personnel, and that people regularly asked him for this information.

Go to Interpreneur.com/resources to get extra materials and free Internet Marketing training

For Step Two I showed him how to set up a simple website, including putting a 'Buy Now' button on it which linked to his Paypal account so he could collect money.

Finally, for Step Three I showed him how to use Google's advertising network to drive targeted traffic to his new site, from people searching for phrases like 'fire service jobs'.

So, in just a couple of hours, I had taught my friend the 'system'. Rick went on and put this into place, and just a few weeks later told me how he was getting a regular income from selling copies of his *'How To Become A Firefighter'* guide every day.

Next I taught him the lesson of 'rinse and repeat' – in other words, once you have a winning formula then you simply do more of the same. Rick's immediate success had proved that people would pay for information about getting a very specific job, so he figured they would probably pay for information about other jobs too. So, Rick then wrote ebooks on how to become a police officer and how to become a paramedic – two of the jobs he already knew plenty about, having worked with a lot of police officers and paramedics over the years.

Trips to gigs with the band now became informal 'mentoring' sessions where Rick would ask me for more tips and strategies on how he could build and grow his business as we drove in the 'band bus' to perform as our Coldplay tribute band. As I learned new things I passed them onto Rick in these sessions and he implemented them. Rick so successfully implemented what I told him that he now has an award-winning business, that has published over 100 career products, and has even expanded beyond the original ebook format which continues to do phenomenally well. As I write this Rick's business - *how2become.co.uk* - has generated sales of almost £5 million!

One of the things I taught Rick was that many of us already have all the necessary knowledge to create an information product in our head, but we just need to recognise this and write it down. A lot of people don't even realise how knowledgeable they are about certain subjects until they actually stop and think, because they are sometimes such an expert in a particular field that it is second nature to them.

That first book of Rick's was packed full of all the knowledge he already had about becoming a firefighter; all he did was turn it into a book and YOU could do something similar. People who possess knowledge that other people would pay for surround us ALL. So, although Rick had never been a police officer or a paramedic he had developed personal friendships with people with these skills through his job. This put him in a position where he could leverage expertise from the people around him to create other products, and this is exactly what he did. You can do the same if you put your mind to it.

As I mentioned earlier, many of my early products actually came from friends, family, neighbours, ex-work colleagues and so on. At this point it's a really good exercise to write out a list of 20 people close to you – they could be friends, work colleagues, relatives, neighbours etc. Just write down the first 20 adults that you know who come to mind. Then, next to each name, write down the job they do now, any jobs you know they have ever done in the past, also any hobbies or interests they may have. This can often be a great catalyst for creating your first product.

Now, I'm not suggesting you simply take this knowledge for free. With friends I would suggest one of two business models – pay them upfront for their knowledge or do a straight 50/50 profit share.

Once you've agreed the payment method you can then work out how best to get the information out of your friend's head and turn it into a product.

For the first model, you could do any, or a combination, of the following:

- Interview them and record answers on a video camera or Dictaphone.

- Video them as they work

- Send them a series of questions that your potential customers would like answering and get them to write their answers down

You would then pull this material into one place and make it available for sale.

If you do the second model, where it is a 50/50 share, your friend would create the product (by doing the steps we've just outlined) and you would provide the website and then do the marketing to get traffic to it. When they provide the content in a product form and you provide the traffic that want to buy it – it's a fair split.

Teaching Rick was really about doing a mate a favour by getting him started. I never thought about teaching and training anybody else, until an opportunity arose to set me on the path to where I am now. Where I began mentoring people to be successful interpreneurs and how this grew to become my *Internet Business School* which you'll hear more about later.

All of my success and the success I was starting to share with others brought me a new task; deciding what to do with all of the money I'd made so far.

LESSON TIME! Simon Says:

Be optimistic when thinking up business ideas – it's easier than you think, and you are probably a lot better connected and clued up than you think you are.

Use your contacts, treat them fairly and everybody wins.

Don't be afraid to ask a friend or neighbour if they are interested in joining you in your business idea – often their enthusiasm will surprise you.

Go to Interpreneur.com/resources to get extra materials and free Internet Marketing training

Use this table to get you started – it's one of the exercises I use at Internet Business School.

Name	Current job, previous job, hobbies, interests.
You	
Friend 1	
Friend 2	
Friend 3 . . .	

CASE STUDY

Tim Kitchen

exposureninja.com

After leaving university I decided to make a go of professional drumming. I spent a couple of years developing something called 'online session drumming', where I'd record for bands and musicians around the world from my home studio. To do this, I had to learn to market myself effectively by building websites, getting to the top of Google, and learning how to advertise.

It turned out that I quite enjoyed the advertising and websites bit of the job, even when I got bored of the drumming. My next door neighbour at the time was a plasterer in need of extra work so I built him a website after watching some online training from Simon and *Internet Business School,* which showed how to do local business marketing. The effect this website had on my next door neighbour spurred me to start *JobDoneWebsites*, which went on to become the UK's leading tradesman-only marketing company.

Next I wrote a book called *How To Get To The Top Of Google,* written because I was fed up reading such basic SEO books full of boring regurgitation about what *not* to do. As this book became increasingly popular (improving the cover design got it on bestseller lists), the volume of enquiries the book generated surpassed what I and my small team could handle. This rapid growth and expansion then led to the creation of my digital marketing agency, Exposure Ninja, which I set up in September 2012. I subsequently enrolled in Simon's mentoring programme and that helped me take my business to the next level.

More books followed and as Exposure Ninja's profile has grown, we've been hiring quickly to keep up. We opened an office in

Nottingham to use as a meeting and training space, although we nearly all work from home as we've found productivity to be significantly higher.

For me personally these last few years have been a lot of fun. In four years we've grown from 1 to 70 people, and learning to run a 70-person company having never had a 'proper' job has meant lots of trials and my fair share of error! Our turnover is over £1 million and growing all the time.

I have a lot to be thankful to Simon for. It was watching his online training that helped me start on my journey, and Exposure Ninja now turns over more each day than I did each month before coming across Simon's training. My company now works with some of his businesses to do their web design and digital marketing, and it's an honour to be involved with an organisation like *Internet Business School* which is helping so many people to get started and make money online.

CHAPTER 11

Going Up In The World?

With the business growing so fast I had put a lot of money into extending my house. The first home improvements started just three months after I left BT and got my yellow Porsche. I just carried on upgrading the house, doing more and more building work, until a couple of years later I'd almost doubled my house by adding seven rooms to it.

However, despite it now being a large property, my home was still a fairly ordinary house in a suburban close (near to at least one neighbour who didn't seem to like me!). So I started thinking about moving out into something a bit grander.

People often talk about 'vision boards' where you put together a montage of images of things you aspire to owning. I never actually created a physical vision board, but in my mind I had this very clear idea of a large country house with a private drive, electric gates and a triple garage. I also really wanted a water feature – either a lake or perhaps river frontage. That was my dream home.

I realise now that the Enid Blyton books I read as a child also influenced my 'vision'. I loved the idea of being able to roam in the open, unspoilt countryside and I dreamed of having Collie dogs bounding around, of listening to birds in the trees and being able to sit by a river or lake to watch the sun rise and set. We're all products of our childhoods, and the *Famous 5* books definitely made a lasting impression on me. I'd done the London commute, been squashed on a tube and breathed in polluted city air. It was time to make my dreams a reality and live the life I really wanted, not the old life I'd been slavishly sucked into and held on to even when it was making me stressed and exhausted.

In terms of location there was a TV series in the early-90s called *The Darling Buds of May* that I loved and had never forgotten. No doubt many of you will remember it too, it starred Sir David Jason (Del Boy from *Only Fools and Horses*) as the patriarch Pop Larkin, Pam Ferris as his wife 'Ma', and then an unknown, up-and-coming actress called Catherine Zeta Jones, who played their eldest daughter Mariette.

The series was set in the heart of 1950s Kent and it portrayed an idyllic lifestyle with the jovial Larkin family enjoying the glorious countryside without a care in the world. I used to watch it on a Sunday night, drinking tea with my granny and completely escaping into the carefree world the lucky Larkin family inhabited.

The TV show was filmed around the village of Pluckley, which was about 30 miles from where I was born and brought up, so when I decided to move house I headed to this little corner of the Garden of England to start my property search there.

I quickly found what seemed to be the perfect property. The Great Barn was a huge converted barn of about 3,500 square feet with separate outbuildings, several acres of land, the triple garage, a long private drive and even the electric gates. The price? A snip at about £800,000. The barn was only half a mile from the farm where the fictional Larkin family lived and *The Darling Buds of May* had been filmed, and best of all it had hundreds of metres of frontage to the River Beult, which meandered through its grounds. I'd almost decided I wanted to buy this fantastic property before I viewed it. As I suspected, the viewing just confirmed it was the dream house I sensed it was, so I agreed the price (yes, I got a discount on the asking price, of course!) and the deal was done. I could not have been happier or more excited – this was what life was all about.

A little more than three years on from when I had taken my redundancy and started my various Internet businesses, here I was moving into a house worth 4x more than my previous home. The Great Barn was amazing and I enjoyed so many new experiences when I started living right out in the countryside. I began feeding the wild ducks, who became increasingly brave and soon began tapping on the door with their beaks to be fed. If the doors were left open they would just walk straight into the house, looking for food!

I had a decking area built out over the river, it was beautiful to just sit there, often watching the swallows and kingfishers. Rabbits would graze on the lawn each evening, moles would also try and ruin that same lawn, and foxes and badgers became regular visitors. In short, this was everything I'd dreamed a country idyll would be, and I was living the way the fictional characters I grew up with had portrayed this kind of lifestyle. *You can see pictures of 'The Great Barn' in the picture section – I sometimes show them to students or when I give talks, to demonstrate how I climbed up the property ladder and to show what you can achieve when you put your mind to it.*

You may have noticed that I've been writing about the barn in the past tense, and that's because after I'd lived there for five years another property came up for sale that I simply couldn't resist. I'll tell you a lot more about that later!

As the business continued to do well and the money was coming in, I decided the clever thing to do would be to not stop at a luxury home upgrade, instead I'd also put some of my profits into investment properties. This seemed a smarter alternative to leaving my money in the bank at a low interest rate. The question was, where was a good place to buy? I'd obviously already purchased the little house in Bulgaria, but with my new-found status I wanted a really nice place in the sun that was a bit swankier than that little £5,000 investment property! I've still got the Bulgaria house, by the way, although I've still never been to Bulgaria!

Spain appealed to me, and as luck would have it (or maybe not, as you will find out when you read on!), I was in possession of a lot of interesting information about which regions were up-and-coming in Spain, and would therefore not just provide me with the sunshine retreat I fancied owning but would be a sound investment opportunity too.

Let me tell you how I came to have this information about Spanish property opportunities. On the back on my original ebook guides on Bulgaria and the like I'd eventually hit on the idea of holding a seminar on investing in property abroad. My thinking was that if I gathered together some interested potential investors and provided some expert speakers on the subject, I would ultimately benefit as my property investment guides could be sold at the end of the talks. Maybe I'd even make a bit of money by organising the seminar and selling tickets? I decided to give it a try.

Remember I told you how the *Business Opportunity Review* website ended up being a 'lead generator' when I stopped charging for memberships? And that I had a sizeable mailing list from that? Well, here's what I did. I combined the list of people who were 'potential investor' contacts from *Business Opportunity Review* with all the contacts who had purchased one of my property guides in the past. This meant I had a very relevant mailing list of potential customers who might be interested in coming to a seminar about investing in property abroad. It was a simple sum: people looking for business opportunities + people interested in property abroad = ideal people to invite to a seminar on property investment opportunities overseas.

Next, I emailed everyone on this mailing list and asked them to take part in a survey, explaining that I was thinking of putting on a seminar in investing in property abroad, and asking if they would be interested in attending. If so, what topics where they interested in? Buy to let? Buying a second home? 100% financing? Buying off plan?

I also asked my potential attendees which countries they may be interested in, which day would best suit them to attend a seminar in the UK, and where they would prefer it to be held. I gave three choices – Heathrow, central London and Birmingham - and I suggested various days of the week. I also asked how much they would be prepared to pay to attend a seminar: Up to £97, £97-£297, £297-£497 or more, up to a maximum of £2,000?

I got a good response and when the results of the survey came back I had a clear winner - a Saturday in Heathrow. Interestingly the majority of the respondents had not gone for the cheapest option, as the most popular price band chosen was £297-£497.

From the number of replies I received I felt confident that I had enough interested parties to make this worth doing, so then I used Google to find some expert property investment speakers to talk at the event. Delivering a speech on this subject was not something I was qualified to do myself, as I only owned my house in Kent and the Bulgaria property I'd got my friend to buy for me. I'd decided to charge £297 a head, and of course I wanted to offer great value for money and find the best speakers I possibly could.

I soon found out the speaking circuit has various different ways of operating. Sometimes speakers are asked to give a talk for free and in return they are allowed to; plug a product, sell it at the back of the room at the end, and of course give out their business card, leaflets and so on. Others are paid a fee and aren't allowed to sell anything.

As this was my first foray into arranging a seminar I was unsure how much money I was going to make, so I decided to ask the speakers to do it for free in return for the chance to make a pitch to sell something. My thinking was that even if a speaker sold just one property to my estimated audience of 60-80 people it would be worth their while, as we were talking about investments of tens or even hundreds of thousands of pounds.

I also had my overheads to consider. Hiring a function room in a hotel at Heathrow was going to cost me around £2,000, and I'd of course pick up the bill for the teas and coffees. I also offered to pay for the speakers' accommodation the night before, to ensure they arrived rested and on time.

I found four speakers who were all experts in their field, explained the deal and got them on board. I cringe now when I think of this, but I asked all of them to come and do their speech for me, in an empty room, so I could make sure they were going to deliver what I wanted them to. It seems a bit rude now, but none of them quibbled and they all did their talk to me, for nothing. I gave them a few pointers about improving their presentation for my audience, and we were all set to go.

I sold 70 tickets, so on the day I took just short of £21,000 on the door – crazy! With my costs at well under £3,000 this had been a great (and somewhat unexpected) commercial success for me. I got fantastic feedback from the audience and the speakers - everyone was happy - even the hotel who had made money through me using their function room and accommodating the speakers. I have since taught this method to lots of students I've mentored, many of whom have used this 'sales funnel' model very successfully in other businesses.

However, despite my success that day, I admit that when I stood up to introduce the speakers and welcome people to the event I was absolutely terrified. I'd never done public speaking like this before and I was a nervous wreck. Still, a few shredded nerves were a small price to pay for this success. I was buzzing when it was finally all over, and to bring me back to my original point, I had also got excited about a property market that one of the speakers had talked enthusiastically about.

This particular speaker explained that the region of Murcia in Spain was underdeveloped at that time, I think as a result of some sort of political dispute that had hampered investment in the area. This situation had been resolved now and so Murcia was ripe for investment. Property prices were already up 23% and were rising as more money was being invested in housing. What's more, as a previously underdeveloped area, Murcia was relatively unspoilt compared to many of the popular British enclaves in other parts of Spain. It sounded like the ideal place to invest and my ears pricked up. Murcia is in south-eastern Spain, and the climate is fantastic. This was exactly the sort of location I'd like to invest in myself, I thought.

So once I was installed in my plush new home in the Kent countryside, had the seminar success under my belt, I decided to buy a place in Murcia, because isn't that what a successful businessman does? Of course, I needed a house in Spain!

I went out to Murcia on a viewing visit and purchased a 4-bedroom villa off-plan, complete with its own private pool and looking straight out over a golf course (even though I don't play golf!). It was in a great location, with views over a lake too, and when I went out there for the first time for a holiday I absolutely loved it. The villa set me back €480,000 and I thought I'd made a great purchase and was very pleased with myself. After all, this was in the heart of a region that was going places. This was a great investment. Right? WRONG!

I eventually went out on holiday about five or six times, but to be honest I got bored. I'd enjoyed the house with its lovely big pool and sun terrace. The weather was fabulous and I enjoyed exploring the region, eating Spanish food and watching the sun set with a glass of sangria in my hand. But once I'd done that, not once but half a dozen times, I'd done it. I was DONE with it!

I decided to rent the place out when I wasn't there, and in the first year it was occupied for 18 weeks. The next year I rented it out for 12 weeks, and then what happened? The crash, that's what happened. It was 2008. Spain was in recession and so was the UK. After that I struggled to rent the villa out for four weeks a year, then two, then not even a single week.

With the house standing unoccupied, guess what happened next? It got burgled, twice. They nicked the TV and DVD player, even the pool pump and the solar panels off the roof. Locals thought the place had been repossessed, as that had happened to a lot of neighbouring properties, so it was open season on my empty villa.

I still own the property, but today it's only worth around €200,000 Ultimately it cost me around €300,000 for what amounted to six holidays in the sun. It's now let out to a long-term tenant. By the way, I don't blame the speaker at my seminar who put in my head the idea of buying in Murcia. He'd have needed a crystal ball to predict the extent of the economic crash and how it would affect the region, but I have learned lessons.

The big lesson is that you should not fall into the trap of thinking you 'should' have a property in the sun. We're conditioned to think this is a great status symbol we should aspire to, but think carefully about how you want to spend your holidays and hard-earned leisure time. If you're like me and you get bored of visiting the same place over and over again, then just hire holiday homes as and when you want them, instead of buying one. There's a lot less hassle involved, and if the economic climate changes, you don't have the headaches I've had.

A few years before the crash I also decided to invest in some unit trusts. I bought four, putting a total of £30,000 in to see what would come of it. Unfortunately, when the crash happened the value of my funds halved in a year, so that was another lesson learned. Dabbling in stocks and shares and unit trusts is a risky business, and you have to be prepared for the fact that while you might get lucky and make a killing, equally you might lose a substantial amount of your investment.

I have no regrets because I wanted to try my hand on the stock market and see where it took me, and I was in the fortunate position that it was not the end of the world for me to lose £30,000. Having said that, I'd still think long and hard about investing in unit trusts again. We've had one almighty crash and we could have another, so is it worth the risk?

LESSON TIME! Simon Says:

Value your contacts and mailing lists. These are ASSETS and you can use them to generate more business, to start a new venture or to create a 'sales funnel'.

Surveys are free to do and give you priceless information about what your customers want, making them much more likely to buy from you. Use them.

Know your personal limits and always give your customers value for money. If that means bringing in experts to help you out, do it.

Don't assume you will have to pay an expert or speaker. Research the market and find out what is expected – for example, giving a speaker an opportunity to sell can be far more valuable to them than a flat fee.

When it comes to purchasing that 'must have' dream property in the sun, stop and think about what this means. Are you attracted by the status symbol or do you REALLY want a base abroad, and to revisit the same place over and over again?

When it comes to buying stocks and shares you need to ask yourself this: can I afford to lose this money? If you can't, you need to invest in something less risky.

CASE STUDY

Francis Dolley

Multiletcashflowsystem.com

After hearing Simon speak at various training events, and sitting beside him at a business breakfast, he inspired me to create an independent business - *The Multi-Let Cashflow System (MLCS).*

'Create a business in a day' Simon said, and we kinda did! 'Future-proof your business career' he said – well I really liked the sound of that!

The business is all about low entry property investment, and essentially teaches people how to take control of multi-let properties to create multiple income streams. Our big promise is to help people replace their income within 12 months, with a completely leveraged property business.

Before I created MLCS I had been self-employed, working in the construction industry. I had a small team of guys working for me but became very disillusioned and frustrated as the years went grinding past. My energy levels dropped and then in the same year I lost my beloved mother to cancer, my sister was diagnosed with a terminal illness and I nearly went bankrupt due to problems on our biggest construction project to date. That was when I decided something had to change.

I did some training and presenting for another company in the property investment sector in 2010-2011, but I was struggling from event to event at first, not making much money. Then, inspired by Simon, I started running my own events and created my online presence. This was a big leap for me - I had considered going it alone for some time, but all the logistics and the work involved made it look too risky.

After following Simon's advice – all picked up from hearing him talk, and subscribing to his newsletters and emails - my wife and I initially went on to host four property investment events in 14 days, with 170 paying customers. As well as making money from day one, I was now also able to employ staff to take the workload away from me. Our mini manuals sell very well from the website, and the day we launched the Systems Masterclass manual we made over £12,000 in sales.

Using Simon's tried and tested methods, and changing the direction of my business has meant an infinitely better lifestyle for my family. Based in Somerset, I now work full time on MLCS with my wife Jane and grown-up children Emily and James, who are both financially independent. In fact, Emily just got married and paid for her own honeymoon in the Caribbean, which made me very happy indeed! Plus, I have just bought my wife Jane a brand new car, something I could NEVER have done in my previous life.

I love the fact MLCS has also given life-changing financial freedom to our countless students, who we call the MLCS family. We have had over 850 people through our training, many of whom are doing amazingly well, some earning in excess of £12k a month.

I would advise others to plug into Simon's world. He walks the walk and his systems work. Just do it!

CHAPTER 12

Office Politics

Another thing I did around the time I was buying the place in Spain and dabbling with stocks and shares was to move into purpose-built business premises. I had no choice after the council had raided my house and told me I had to stop running the business from home!

Anyhow, in a way I reckoned the neighbours and council officials had probably done me a favour. Despite the addition of air-conditioning, the truth was I'd reached the point where I felt it would be fitting to have a rather fancier place to call my office than a spare room stuffed with desks, so I embraced the challenge of branching out into proper office space.

The first thing I did was decide to buy rather than rent. This was an easy decision as quite simply I'd looked at rental prices and realised I could buy an office for less than the cost of the rent. I spoke to my accountant who advised me that from a tax perspective, because commercial buildings can be held in pension schemes, this would be a doubly good idea. I could put money into a pension to buy a building, and that pension contribution would be free of tax. So far so good.

I started looking around and found a new building that was 1,500 square foot on a purpose-built business park in Ashford. It seemed perfect. It had two floors and I could easily house the six staff I now had working for me, plus I would still have room for expansion. In the meantime I could rent out the spare space until I needed it. So, the luxury HQ was purchased at a cost of £320,000. I was delighted. My premises had their own reception area and even a boardroom! Suddenly I was feeling very corporate and I was looking forward to hosting meetings at my posh new control centre.

However, I did have some unexpected bills to pay. It cost me about £20,000 I hadn't anticipated just to get the HQ up and functioning. The building I purchased was just a shell and it cost £6,000 to put sockets in with the required floor boxes, £7,000 for office partitioning and another few £2-3,000 for the kitchen facilities. Plus I had to find ANOTHER £60,000 to pay my VAT bill on the building. I could claim that back on my next tax return of course, but to be honest this left me with a bit of a cash flow issue. Nevertheless I stayed optimistic. It would all be worth it in the end, because these new premises were going to help me grow my business and make life a lot easier for me. That was the theory, in any case.

Then I found the business rates on the premises were over £1,000 per month which, taken together with the other costs, meant the office building was costing around £3,400 per month to operate, when you included the rates, mortgage, service charges and utility bills. No wonder the council is so hot on stopping people operating businesses from their homes! I'd had no idea how much money I was accidentally saving when I had everything running from my spare room.

Anyhow, I have to admit I did enjoy the luxury and the kudos of owning the fancy office, and my various Internet businesses were of course still doing very well indeed so I could afford the premises. However, in time some complications started to appear with this business empire I had created.

At the peak I had ten people working for me, and one day I looked around and to my horror I was reminded of working back at BT! Here I was dressed in a shirt and jacket, back in the corporate world and effectively managing a team. With that came the inevitable human problems you face with any workforce.

I had people going off sick – one in particular did for several months - co-workers falling out with each other, and I even had an employee stealing from me. I kid you not! This happened in 2008, a year or so after I'd started to run my *Internet Business School.* One of the services I offered to students was help in building websites for their businesses. This one particular employee was responsible for designing the websites, and unfortunately I found out that he was doing backhanders by offering to build the sites for half price if customers contacted him secretly, via his private Hotmail account. To add insult to injury when I found this out and sacked him I asked him to return his laptop – then I discovered that the case was stuffed with teabags and toilet rolls that he'd also been stealing from me!

After that I took a deep breath and looked around my premises. Did I really want all these headaches? How big did I want my business to be? This felt too complicated and too big, but where was the sweet spot? I didn't really know, but I knew what I DIDN'T want. I didn't want to be sucked back into the corporate world I'd left behind when I quit my job with BT. I didn't want office politics, I didn't want to manage all these people and I didn't want the hassle of either buying teabags and toilet rolls OR having them nicked off me! What had I done?

Probably the only really good thing about the premises was that I eventually ran various courses and classes for the business school in the space upstairs. This worked and saved money on hotel conference rooms, which ultimately made me stick with this flash HQ for about three years in total.

In all I was running four strands of my business from my premises. The first was my basic 'info products', like my books on plastering, electrical regulations and home staging. The second was an extension of the info products business, selling 'higher ticket' info products, such as the plumbing course. Then I had *Business Opportunity Review,* and finally my newest business – the *Internet Business School.*

As ever, I learned lessons from this latest experience of buying property, some of which have been reiterated in other property deals I'd been involved in.

LESSON TIME! Simon Says:

Always check ALL costs. Look out for things you don't immediately think of, such as VAT on commercial buildings and business rates costs (even if a building is empty these still have to be paid).

If you buy something leasehold check the service charges as often these are over the top and can eat into a significant amount of your

My school photo at Meopham
Junior School, aged 10

The house I grew up in on Lynton
Road South, Gravesend

My first business delivering leaflets, aged 11

207 Old Street London, where I worked for BT for
many years and my BT staff ID card, circa 1995

The actual copy of 'The Beermat Entrepreneur'
that I purchased on the day I left BT

Attending my first ever workshop on
Information Products, December 2003

My first product - the Bulgaria Property Guide

My early Information Products, 2006

Early Coolplay gig 2005

The Coolplay tour bus - purchased with the majority of my redundancy money

Coolplay gig Narberth Wales 2006

The Coolplay website - the UK's No 1 (and only) Coldplay Tribute Band

Performing to 40,000 people at the V Festival site, Hylands Park Chelmsford, with Coolplay in 2007

Coolplay gig 2014 Sussex

Dan Slowly, Me, Richard McMunn and Steve Jenner - My besties to this day; performing as Coolplay in Guernsey 2015

View from Coolplay gig Guernsey August 2016

The range of products grows...

Another busy day of orders, 7 sacks full of information products on CDs and DVDs to post

A good day! Orders ready for collection, each box has sold for £495!

The Porsche I purchased after 3 months of starting my business in 2004. Nice colour!

My house (inset) when I started, and then after the huge extension on the same house!

My first ever speaking gig, 2006

The view from the stage at Bournemouth Conference Centre for my third speaking gig, 2007

The Great Barn, which I purchased in 2007

Me outside The Great Barn

Me being filmed by Channel 4 for 'The Secret Millionaire'

The corporate office building that I purchased in Ashford, after the visit from the council

Dinner with the Dragons - don't blink!

Meeting Peter Jones at a charity ball - I said don't blink!

Blenheim Palace Ball with Duncan Bannatyne

Meeting Theo Papahitis at another posh do - and my eyes are finally open!

rental. I once bought a one-bed flat in Leeds to rent out at £550 per month, but the service charges were over £150 a month, only giving me a yield of about 3% on the money I invested in it. To cap it all the apartment block flooded, a burglar kicked in the front door and the boiler packed up after 18 months!

If you're buying something to rent out, try renting it BEFORE you own it and don't rely on what estate agents tell you. Simply place an ad to try renting it out and see if the phone rings.

If you rent out a luxury property don't add a hot tub! In recent times I had a seaside place in the UK, at Whitstable in Kent. I had a succession of tenants who turned the water brown with fake tan, spilt red wine in the tub and clogged up the filters with grass. Every turnaround required a full drain, clean and refill of the tub. This takes several hours to do and costs money. Basically, when people rent something they fundamentally don't take care of the property as if it was their own.

The most important lesson of all is to stop and think about exactly what you are taking on. Imagine yourself as boss of your new building. What will your working day be like? Will you have to be governed by your alarm clock every morning, like you were in your old job? How many people will you have working for you and do you want that responsibility?

I am currently turning over £1 million a year with a staff of two as everything else is outsourced. It's quite a nice metric, plus I get to work from home and I get up when I wake up instead of when the alarm clock tells me I need to get ready for the office – is this the sort of set-up you would prefer?

CASE STUDY

Jay Hastings

AskJayHastings.com

After having a few private mentoring sessions with Simon I did his 3-day Internet marketing workshop in 2012. I previously had a career in customer service management for Royal Bank Of Scotland, followed by another team management role at a large housing association.

I had tried a number of things over the years to help me become financially free (including enrolling on online courses from so-called American 'gurus') but nothing worked. I was attracted to Internet marketing, having seen lots of people on YouTube claiming they made money whilst sleeping, and that's why I got in touch with Simon.

Internet Business School has completely transformed my life. I went from earning just over £30k in a day job to £94k in my first year, and since then I have continued to grow my 6 figure income, which has completely changed life for my family and me. I've done this through a variety of means, from joint ventures in Internet businesses to affiliate marketing and taking on local business clients. What's more, the results were quick and I was making money within three weeks!

The flexibility I have in my working life is absolutely fantastic. I'm 35 years old and I work whenever I want from my base in South London, for however many hours I choose, whilst still making a very, very decent income. I get to spend as much time as I want with my young daughter Skye and often feel I'm living the dream.

I still have more to achieve in this whole online game, because I believe that if Simon can generate £20 million then so can I! Nevertheless I'm now able to go on luxury holidays to the

Caribbean, I've just ordered a brand new Mercedes Benz, enrolled my daughter into private education and we visit London's top restaurants. The fact alarm clocks and rush hours are a thing of the past is priceless.

Without a doubt, Simon and the *Internet Business School* can change your life. You should try it.

CHAPTER 13

Accidental
Public Speaker

So, let's rewind a little and have a look at how my business was doing in 2007, when I was at the point of moving into the swanky office premises. What shape was the business in? It was in BRILLIANT shape!

Within three years of starting from scratch after leaving BT I had amassed sales of over £2 million from home selling all my various information-based products, and from subscriptions to *Business Opportunity Review.*

Things were already great, and then out of the blue a seminar promoter who was organising a 'wealth creation' seminar approached me with a new and exciting opportunity. He'd seen my *Business Opportunity Review* site and asked me if I'd be willing to send an email to my contacts list to promote his event, on a 50/50 share of ticket revenue. I thought this seemed like a no-brainer. All I had to do was send an email to my mailing list and I'd pick up some easy money, so I agreed and duly sent the promo email to my contacts promoting this guy's seminar.

The organiser was very pleased when I sold quite a few tickets from this, and he called me for a chat. 'Is there anything I can do for you in return?' he asked. He started asking about my business and I explained to him all about my information product empire, and that I was selling ebooks, CDs and DVDs. I told him that was my 'main' business and that it had made over £2 million from it, which he was pretty surprised to hear. 'Blimey, sounds like you should be a SPEAKER at my event not just promoting it!' he exclaimed. 'Do you want to speak and share your story?'

Now at this point I didn't consider myself a speaker at all and had no intention of getting in to that business. When I'd put on the property investment event I'd been absolutely terrified of even standing up and introducing the experts I had lined up to talk, the idea of speaking out myself to a whole room of people really did not appeal. I thought back to the team meetings I had to hold at BT. I'd have to talk to ten people about what my team had done that month and I'd be trembling with nerves!

Go to Interpreneur.com/resources to get extra materials and free Internet Marketing training

Nevertheless, I listened to this guy. He said if I shared with an audience what I had done, then maybe some of them could escape from a job they weren't enjoying in the corporate world just like I had done. I started to feel duty bound, and after some deliberation I eventually decided to give it a go. I think the adventurer inside me wanted to see where this would lead. It was an opportunity, wasn't it? I decided I had nothing to lose, other than a bit of sleep the night before! Also, with the property seminar it was out of the question that I would speak, as I was not an expert in the field. This was very different – nobody was more of an expert than me on my own success story!

In preparation I arranged a few slides that documented the websites I had created, gave examples of the information products I sold and compiled a list of tips on getting traffic to websites. Luckily, I found out only about 30 people would be in the audience (and as I recall about half of those had come from my email list!). This was a relief – it didn't seem like too big an ask and I told myself I could handle it, all had to do was keep calm, believe in myself and look confident.

On the day I took a deep breath and just went for it. I told my story in the way that came naturally to me, despite my nerves. I went for a laid-back, chatty approach and didn't try to do anything flash or overly complicated. I just stuck to the facts about what I'd done and what the results were. I was self-effacing and even self-deprecating at times. The feedback I got later was that this came as a pleasant surprise to the delegates, as speakers talking about their successful business enterprises often have a bit of an ego or an arrogant streak that gets in the way and can irritate people.

I spoke for just over an hour before thanking the audience and walking off stage to warm applause. To my surprise, at that moment the promoter came running up to me saying 'where's your offer, where's your offer?' I didn't know what he meant. What was I supposed to do - sell them an ebook on Bulgaria property investment, or a plumbing course? The promoter politely pointed out the way the seminar business worked was that speakers are expected to make an offer to sell something at the end of their presentation. Now I got the basic logic of this – after all I'd got the property experts to speak on the basis they could make a pitch to the audience to promote their businesses. However, what I learned now was that ticket sales alone for seminars rarely cover the venue costs, and so speakers are expected to pay a commission to the seminar promoter from whatever they sell at the end. Silly me!

It was a bit awkward as I was not prepared for this and had no offer to make, so I just apologised and said that I hadn't realised I was supposed to sell something. It was nobody's fault - this had simply been a miscommunication between us. The upshot was that we agreed that I'd speak again at this guy's next event (it seemed the audience had loved my real life story), and that in the meantime I'd prepare something to sell in the form of coaching/training sessions. These, I worked out, should be sessions similar to those I'd provided to Rick the fireman, to help others get their own Internet businesses started up along the same lines.

Around three months later I spoke at the next event, this time to a slighter bigger audience of 40 people. At the end of my presentation I offered to provide 10 x hour-long mentoring sessions to anyone who wanted my help in getting started in an Internet business, all for a price of £995. It seemed a lot to sell my time for very nearly £100 an hour, but it was what people prepared to pay and, even though it surprised me, this was what my time and expertise had become worth.

The promoter and I were both very pleased when three members of the audience took up the offer. This meant I had generated £3,000 worth of business in under 90 minutes. Of course, I had to pay a commission to the seminar promoter and provide a total of 30 hours of 1:1 coaching, but nevertheless this was still well under a week's work in man hours – and it was a much better rate than I used to earn at BT! I mean, if I could do that every week I'd be earning an extra £12,000 a month in addition to the money coming in from information products!

I did most of the 1:1 sessions on Skype. I found I enjoyed delivering the lessons and it came quite naturally to me, which was another big bonus. It was very satisfying to help people turn their ideas into cash, and there are loads of highly successful businesses that developed through people coming on my courses. Two of the early successes were:

Thierry, a Frenchman, who had the unlikely idea of selling tins of snail caviar. He had tasted it at a dinner party and enjoyed it, and I helped him set up a profitable business as an online reseller for the product.

Bill Goldie, who is featured earlier in this book as a case study and whose daughter suffered from Osgood Schlatter disease. As Bill has described he wrote a successful manual to help other families dealing with OSD and has generated over £200,000 to date.

When I established Internet Business School to develop my mentoring and coaching courses the success stories multiplied. They include:

A woman who specialised in the application of permanent make-up and ended up teaching other beauticians how to do it, turning over £30,000 a month through her training courses.

A woman who got an outsourcer to put together courses on subjects like mindfulness which she then sold on Groupon, making £20,000 a month. (Remember what I said about catching the wave with a 'nice-to-have' product – this was one of those businesses, as she launched the book when mindfulness and so on were suddenly all the rage).

Ben Brophy, who was friends with the ex-Radio 1 DJ Danny Rampling, wrote an ebook guide with Danny on how to become a DJ. On the back of this they got a mainstream publishing deal that made them both money, revamping Danny's career in the process. Ben is featured as a case study at the end of this chapter.

Through the seminars I did, and by coaching these budding entrepreneurs, I realised I had stumbled into a new business area –

that of Internet marketing. If I could market my courses and myself I could have another massively lucrative business on my hands.

I found out there was a huge seminar being held in Atlanta on exactly this topic - in fact, it was billed as the biggest Internet marketing seminar in the world. To stay ahead of the curve I knew I needed to learn the latest strategies and tips from America, where they were 6 to 12 months ahead of the UK. I think it's very important to keep educating yourself and looking forward. Even though I had a lot of successful businesses already under my belt, in no way did I want to sit on my butt and spend my days watching Jeremy Kyle, funny cat videos or epic falls on YouTube.

I believe very strongly that you need to make hay while the sun shines – and the sun was certainly shining on me.

I considered it a sound investment to buy a flight and take myself out to Atlanta to learn as much as I could about Internet marketing, and to this day I have never stopped educating myself as much as I possibly can. So far I have spent in the region of £250,000 on educating myself through various courses and seminars on everything from Google AdWords to 'how to improve your entrepreneurial mindset' type talks, which are always motivational although sometimes a bit on the 'happy-clappy' side for my liking!

Anyhow, being an ambitious, knowledge-hungry Interpreneur, I flew to this event in Atlanta feeling optimistic and very keen and excited to learn more about Internet marketing. The seminar didn't disappoint and was extremely informative, and as luck would have it, while I was there I got a break that ultimately turned out to be far more valuable to me than the content of the talks – and that was very good indeed!

Remember when I left BT and I attended that first seminar, given by Andrew Reynolds, the guy who introduced me to the idea of selling information products? Well, guess who I bumped into during one of the breaks at this massive seminar? You guessed it – there was Andrew. Somewhat embarrassingly we bumped into each other in the gents toilets, of all places! He clearly didn't recognise me at all, but I made myself known, shook his hand and thanked him for setting me on this path that had generated £2 million pounds by 2007, a sum that was rising fast.

Andrew was pleased to meet a successful student and wanted to know more about how I had achieved this, so we agreed to meet up when both back in the UK a couple of weeks later. At this meeting I gave Andrew an overview of the products I'd sold and told him that I had recently become a speaker at seminars myself (failing to mention my career spanned just two small events and that the first time I'd made a bit of hash of things without selling anything!).

Andrew told me he was organising another event himself a few months later and asked if I'd be willing to speak at his seminar and share my success story, possibly offering mentoring as my 'offer' as I had done at my last talk. I quickly accepted his kind offer, hoping the event he was planning would be larger than my previous outings to 30 to 40 people, thereby potentially making it even more profitable for me. From memory, the original seminar of Andrew's I'd been to a few years earlier was for about 100 people, and I hoped this one would be of a similar size. After all, I'd sold three mentoring packages after speaking to 40 people, so presumably I could sell at least double that to an audience of 100.

Andrew gave me the date, which I put in my diary, and then I just waited to hear some more details nearer the time.

Some weeks later I got an email from Andrew with a photograph attached. The picture was taken from the stage at the Bournemouth International Conference Centre and showed 3,500 empty seats. The email said: 'This is the view from the stage at the event I'm planning, are you still up for it?' You can see the actual picture he sent in the photo section, to see for yourself how daunting this was!

I gulped and felt my heart skip a beat, and in hindsight this has become one of those pivotal moments in my life. Adrenalin flooded through me; should I flee, or fight? The decision I made here would ultimately affect much of the journey I'll go on to describe in the rest of the chapters in this book. In that scary moment I could have fled and 'bottled it' – after all this was to be my third ever public speaking gig and Andrew was suggesting I do it to an audience 100 times bigger than I was used to. But I didn't, of course I didn't!

Instead I took a deep breath and thought 'Come on Simon, you can do it!' I told myself that essentially I would be giving the same presentation that I had already successfully delivered twice. I didn't have to change what I did; it was just that the audience would be bigger. It was all in my mind. I could do it - I just had to tell myself nothing was different. Simple, wasn't it? Well, I would soon find out the answer!

My fingers were shaking over the keyboard when I typed my response.

'Fine, no problems,' I told Andrew, and that was it. There was no going back – I'd chosen to 'fight' and I was committed to going through with it.

When the day of the seminar came I was incredibly nervous, so much so that my memories of actually delivering my talk are a bit blurred. I did it though, and I did it reasonably well, unbelievably. Even so, when I look back at a video of the event now I laugh. Having never taken any public speaking training and having very little experience, the night before the event (well prepared as ever!) I'd been looking on Google for training and advice on being a speaker. It seemed there was a general consensus of opinion that maintaining eye contact with the audience was essential. I read that speakers should look around the room and try and connect with everyone. Of course, 7,000 eyes looking up at me on the stage was a lot of contact to try to make, so during my presentation I constantly walked across the stage from one side to the other, scanning the audiences from left to right and top to bottom, trying to make sure I looked at each of the 3,500 attendees regularly (though only for a nanosecond!).

Anyway, I have forgiven myself for my poor technique, because at the end of my presentation I offered 10 x 1:1 sessions of Internet marketing coaching for £1,997 each – and to my delight I got 86 customers. That generated revenue of over £170,000 in 90 minutes – and so perhaps you won't be surprised to learn that my fear of public speaking was suddenly cured! 'Bring it on,' I thought. 'I definitely CAN do it!'

I started working with these new coaching students and found that I could quickly show them how to start an online business that generated significant incomes for themselves. Amongst the students from this event was Keith, an ex-haulage contractor, who I coached to set up a business selling a training course and manual on getting the Certificate of Professional Competence, which enables you to obtain your CPC in Road Haulage to operate HGV vehicles. He quickly turned this into a business that generates an average of £1,500 a month and has made him at least £135,000 profit.

Another student, Mat, was only 16, and his dad paid for him to do the course. He didn't have an idea of what to sell, but I taught him how to find ideas from newspapers and he went on to set up a business selling a guide on keeping bees. He created an ebook and quickly started making more than £3,000 a month from it.

With a string of successes under my belt I decided to set up a new company specialising in this area, and this is where I finally get to tell you about *Internet Business School.* This new company, whilst secondary to my core business of selling products, would handle the new revenue stream created from teaching the skills that I had been developing, namely identifying the ways of making money online, finding in demand markets and getting traffic to websites.

While I was delivering the coaching I'd already sold in Bournemouth – 86 students was quite a lot to provide for! – I didn't seek out more speaking engagements, but I found that other seminar organisers were approaching me based on my earlier appearances. I was on their radar and on the circuit, it seemed, and so eventually I started doing an average of about 5-10 speaking gigs a year and mentoring students to repeat my success following my baptism of fire at the Bournemouth International Conference Centre.

Over time I found that a more effective use of time in teaching students who came to *Internet Business School* was to actually run a classroom-based training course for a small group, rather than working 1:1. So, since around 2007, I've run a handful of courses each year to teach the techniques I use in my other Internet companies. This is where my business premises actually did come in useful, because from 2008-2010 I ran these courses from the upstairs classroom offices in my fancy office space.

I've discovered that Internet marketing has to be the fastest-moving business there is with the never-ending changes from Google, Facebook and newer platforms like Snapchat. Still, today, I'm continually learning and attending seminars, and in my courses I reflect the latest strategies that are working right now. When I run the course the material changes EVERY time, because changes are happening every week – and this means the demand for courses goes on and on.

To date *Internet Business School* has helped thousands of people get their online business into profit, making tens and hundreds of thousands of pounds and in some cases literally MILLIONS. I've coached people from aged 9-86 and I've helped brand new start-ups right through to established businesses. The best of it is I've really enjoyed applying Internet marketing techniques into a whole range of businesses. Having mentored entrepreneurs in just about every kind of business you can think of, I've actually developed the skill of applying Internet marketing strategies to just about ANY kind of business.

Perhaps the best example I can give you is that of Frankie Widdows, featured earlier in the book as a case study. As she explained, Frankie was a former police dog handler who had the most extreme career change you could imagine when she launched an eyelash extension business. She left the police in 2012 and her business now turns over an eye-popping £400k - £500k per year.

To find out more about my current training courses, go to *InternetBusinessSchool.com*

LESSON TIME! Simon Says:

If you've got nothing to lose except some sleep or a few fingernails from biting them down – GO FOR IT when opportunities arise! It's an old cliché, but you have to be in it to win it and you never know where an opportunity may lead.

BE YOURSELF in all areas of business. It's exhausting playing a version of yourself and you need to put all your energy into what counts - making profits. This is even more important when you are speaking to an audience. People can spot integrity and honesty a mile off so don't try to be somebody you aren't. Respect and support will follow, and people who trust and admire you are more likely to buy from you.

If you make a mistake – as I did by failing to make an offer at that early seminar – hold your hands up and apologise. Nobody is perfect, and you can offer to make amends next time.

Believe in yourself, and know your value. I was surprised to command business that valued my time at £100 an hour, but that was what I was worth and deserved to be paid, and I even doubled that rate within a year.

Feel proud, not embarrassed, by what you are worth and remember that sometimes customers feel happier to pay a higher price as they believe they are getting a better product. (Remember when I did the customer survey asking how much to charge at the property seminar, and the cheapest price didn't win? People are prepared to pay for QUALITY and EXPERTISE.)

Never stop educating yourself. Clearly I didn't have £250,000 to spend on self-improvement when I set out as an Interpreneur, but I've always spent what I could afford over the years as it's crucial to stay sharp and ahead of the game. Education is never, ever wasted. Invest in yourself – you are worth it.

Life is too short for 'what ifs' so when you feel the adrenalin pumping, choose to FIGHT not FLEE. As the saying goes, when you look back on your life you'll regret the things you didn't do more than the things you did!

CASE STUDY

Ben Brophy

www.Ben-Brophy.com

I saw Simon speak at multiple events a number of years ago. What stood him apart from all the other presenters was his down to earth 'guy next door' demeanour combined with the indisputable success he'd clearly attained. Every other speaker kept talking a good game whilst Simon was clearly *playing* a very good game. There's a BIG difference - talk is cheap. Results are what count and it stands him apart from most others.

I invested in training with Simon, subsequently wrote a successful ebook guide with the ex-Radio 1 DJ Danny Rampling on how to become a DJ, and now I'm an online marketing coach, speaker, course facilitator and published author (in print, DVD & online), assisting people and businesses to leverage their skills and resources. I'm 41 and London based.

It was after achieving publishing deals and millions of views for clients on platforms including YouTube that I was invited to speak and train alongside Simon and his *Internet Business School.* I only side with the best in their respected industry and Simon is that man in Internet marketing. Many people come and go whereas Simon is consistently at the front of the pack - investing in new skills, staying ahead of the curve and (most importantly) taking massive, intelligent action.

In my opinion Simon's ability to see opportunities and ways that technology and tools can be used to generate income is uncanny, and that is why he gets to spend time with business leaders such as Sir Richard Branson on Necker Island. Best of all Simon shares all his tried and tested best practice with thousands of people through his programmes and workshops, helping to transform many lives in the process!

I am fortunate in that I have seen every single feedback form after dozens of courses. No other Internet programme or course gets such consistent reviews of '9 out of 10' and '10 out of 10'. The feedback speaks for itself!

The benefits for me have come in lifestyle changes. Simon helped open my mind to a whole world of opportunity and I now enjoy travelling globally, working on projects and sharing skills that I've developed since embarking on the journey alongside Simon. I love speaking and training with exciting people and businesses, and I truly appreciate being able to work remotely. These are the things that matter to me in life, and the future has never been so exciting.

CHAPTER 14

Make It Happen

Following my success at the Bournemouth seminar I was invited to do another big speaking event, this time at the Brighton Centre. My nerves were better this time and my performance much more polished, but nevertheless I nearly fell over when Andrew Reynolds subsequently asked me to speak at an even bigger event – the 'The Entrepreneurs Bootcamp 2009'. This was billed as the 'ultimate event for aspiring millionaires' and would take place at London's O2 Arena. GULP!

I knew the O2 was one of the largest indoor arenas in Europe with a seating capacity of 23,000, and it had recently been named as the world's busiest venue, beating even Madison Square Garden in New York. I really had to pinch myself, because this was the most incredible opportunity ever presented to me. It was very exciting but it also scared the life out of me, and once again I told myself I just had to be myself and do what I'd done before, forgetting about the size of the audience.

I had several months' notice before the big event and on New Year's Eve 2008 I was invited to see Elton John at the O2, spending the evening in one of the posh boxes. I can remember looking around and thinking 'Oh my God! This is terrifying!' I'd never been in one of those boxes before and it gave me a bird's eye view of the huge arena and the stage. It was breathtaking, and when I imagined myself on the stage with my slides; describing how I got made redundant from BT, starting my business from my spare room, buying but never seeing in person the Bulgarian house that inspired this whole new life for me, the hairs on the back of my neck stood up.

Being up in the audience that night also made me think about how I was going to make my talk stand out from the presentations given by all of the other speakers. As the O2 is an expensive venue to hire the organisers would be making full use of the time and had a packed schedule running from 9 a.m. - 9 p.m. over two days, with loads of interesting speakers lined up from all over the world. The speakers all had one thing in common: they were talking about how to make money online, just like me. I started to think very hard about what cards I could play to make my voice heard. Not only was I up against a sea of other people who would also be selling mentoring and training courses at the end of their talk, but I also had to consider that some members of the audience would have seen me speak before, maybe in Bournemouth or Brighton. What could I do differently to keep their interest for my 90 minutes in the spotlight?

For starters I decided to get fantastic glossy leaflets printed up. I was really pleased with them – they were the most impressive leaflets I'd seen – but this wasn't enough. I needed a really big idea, and it suddenly came to me one day when I thought about that stage at the O2.

'Wouldn't it be cool to bring the band out on stage?' I thought. 'What a great thing for us all to do! Imagine Coolplay playing the O2? Now that would really make my performance memorable, and it would be the gig of a lifetime!'

This wasn't a completely crazy idea, as the band had already had a taste of playing to big audiences. In 2007 the Sun newspaper ran a feature on tribute bands as they were growing rapidly in popularity at that time. You see, journalists use Google too, and I'd used my Internet marketing skills to get the band's website on the first page of Google for a number of search phrases relating to tribute bands. The guys and me were asked if we'd be happy to appear in the feature and of course we said yes! We figured any publicity was good publicity, and how right we were.

We got a massive plug as the feature was splashed across two full-pages and only mentioned three other tribute bands. This meant millions of people had potentially heard of Coolplay by now, and straightaway the phone started to ring with offers of all sorts of exciting gigs and opportunities. Ultimately we had a write-up in the NME and a couple of other magazines, plus airtime on Virgin Radio and BBC Radio.

In August 2007 we played at the V Festival site - Hylands Park in

Chelmsford - to a crowd of 40,000, which was awesome. After that we were booked to play to a crowd of 100,000 in Crete, asked to appear a stadium gig in Portugal, and then many other events including shows in Wales and Ireland. We were also booked regularly for tribute band weekends at Butlins, at all of their camps several times a year.

Despite all this success, playing the O2 would still be an incredibly exciting experience and was certainly worth pushing for. It was one of those 'bucket list' things really. I mean, nobody gets to play the O2 unless they're an A-lister, do they? I had to try to make this work – it was a brilliant idea!

Without mentioning it to the guys in the band – I already knew they would snatch my hand off for an opportunity like this so I didn't to run it past them first – I ran my idea past the organiser.

'No, it would be a logistical nightmare,' I was told. 'It's not possible.'

Now then, as a salesman you need to overcome objections in order to close your sale, and in this situation I was effectively being a salesman, trying to flog my brilliant idea to the event organiser. I wasn't going to take no for an answer this readily, so I asked him precisely what the objections were, then I could work out how to overcome them. Once I'd done that and solved the problems, how could he refuse?

I discovered the organisers were building a 110-foot wide screen on stage, the biggest ever used in the O2. On top of this there would be a series of 'repeater screens' hung from the ceiling to give everyone in the audience the best view, and several LED walls were being built under the main screen. Technically it would be very tricky to get the band on and off the stage with all this other kit, and after pushing for information and discussing the logistics at length I found out the only way to do this would be to have the band wheeled onto the stage on 'risers', emerging from backstage as the LED screens were lifted up to reveal the band members arriving on individual podiums.

'It'll cost a fortune,' I was told.

'I'll pay whatever it costs,' I said.

'Right, I'll look into it.'

It turned out the audio-visual company (in charge of the set, stage and all the technical stuff) was very pleased to help, and with me offering to pay for all the extra kit and technicians needed to make this work there were no objections left, at least not from the organiser.

There was one other hurdle to jump, however. The conference was being filmed and DVDs of the event would be sold afterwards. This meant we needed to talk to Coldplay about whether they'd be happy for Coolplay to be recorded singing one of their songs in this way. Unfortunately, it turned out it would cost a massive fee to licence one song! With that I looked at the option of using another band's song, to see if it might be cheaper. I thought of using Take That's 'Greatest Day' but got no reply when I contacted their various different publishers.

This didn't put me off – I think it made me more determined! – and my next thought was to create an original song. Time was ticking now and I tried to think if I had any contacts at all in the songwriting world that might be able to help. Eureka! I knew someone locally who worked with up-and-coming musicians, and I asked her if she knew an artist who could help compose a song for us. She did – between us we created an original track called 'Make It Happen' featuring lyrics about turning dreams into action, which were very appropriate to the audience.

The band was absolutely delighted when I broke the news that this was all happening. They loved the song and we rehearsed it as much as we could, all getting very excited about our forthcoming performance. It was unbelievable that we'd gone from playing to a handful of people in a pub to playing to a crowd of 40,000 at the Hylands Park site, and going on stage at the O2 in just a few short years - 'Make it Happen' we certainly had!

Now I just had to decide where in my presentation I wanted to bring the band on stage. I couldn't do it at the end, as that was when I'd give my pitch to sell the services of my *Internet Business School.* I decided it had to be somewhere in the final third, once I'd had the chance to engage with the audience enough to be able to present them with this somewhat unprecedented little interlude. This of course meant that I'd have to break off from talking – and I'd have been talking for about an hour at the point I was bringing the band on – and then make the switch to singing. It was a big ask but I was really up for it.

We got to do one dry run at the O2, unfortunately the rollers being used to wheel the band on to the stage got stuck – what a nightmare! The guys were cool though, and all of them shrugged this off and said they were sure it would be alright when we did it for real.

On the day itself my nerves were shredded, but I'm happy to say I did manage to take in the enormity of what was happening and I enjoyed every second of it. (If you search YouTube for Simon Coulson O2 you can watch the moment!) I'd brought in an extra guitarist, who's a friend of mine, purely because I knew how much he'd enjoy the experience, and because I could. That's the sort of thing that I really love about the success I'm enjoying. It's not about figures on a balance sheet, it's about being able to do special things, have amazing experiences and really make the most of your life. Seeing the guys enjoying the event and sharing it with them was priceless – and I'll never forget the look on their faces when we got a standing ovation! I'd seen Madonna at the O2 and she didn't get a standing ovation, and here was this pub band getting one!

The talk went well too and I loved delivering it, despite breaking into a sweat and having a runaway beating heart! This time I was selling a comprehensive Internet marketing course for £2,000, and I made more than half a million pounds worth of sales in the 90 minutes, with 263 customers buying a course. This gave them two days in a classroom and 1:1 sessions with me. It had been a huge success, which of course meant that I now had my work well and truly cut out!

After that I had up to a 130 people at a time in the classroom and I was spending an awful lot of time doing the 1:1 business coaching. The plus side was that I was learning a lot about a wide variety of businesses – everything from chiropractic and veterinary services to running bus companies – and this was all very useful in broadening my own education. I was also tweaking the course all the time to keep abreast of Internet technology and new marketing techniques, and in time I changed the structure of the course, to make it better for everyone. It's grown from two days to three days and I've had the school accredited so we can award recognised Level 3 Diplomas in Internet marketing.

The O2 event had been the biggest entrepreneur conference in the UK ever, and word quickly spread about it, all over the world. I was asked to speak at events all around the globe, and for a while I found it was a great way to see the world. For instance, I spoke at conferences twice in Johannesburg, and while I was in South Africa I went on safari. There were opportunities in places like Australia, Dubai, Kuala Lumpur, Slovenia, Ireland and Germany too – so many I couldn't take them all up. This was partly because it was impossible to do everything and it was also a lifestyle choice.

The events I chose to speak at were some of the largest entrepreneur events in the world, and to my surprise I even won an award for being the top speaker at some of them! I'd come a long way in a short space of time, and in time I got to share the stage with some famous faces, including Sir Richard Branson, Lord Alan Sugar, Tony Robbins, Brian Tracy, Bob Proctor – and even former president Bill Clinton. I'll tell you more about my dealings with some of these inspirational people later, and how I learned from the best.

LESSON TIME! Simon Says:

Work out the best way of making your presentation, and if there are obstacles in your way ask yourself how you can overcome them, and do everything you possibly can to make your vision happen.

Accept that you will be nervous when public speaking – it is a nerve-racking experience - but take comfort from the knowledge adrenalin will kick in. I found that adrenalin made me operate on a higher level and in some cases put me on autopilot. The quips come easier when adrenalin is flooding your body, so embrace the temporary stress and use it to your advantage.

Keep your sense of humour. At an event in Dubai I played an introductory video and no sound came out. About 300 people stared at me, watching video with no soundtrack, so I did a spur of the moment fake narration. I was saying things like 'This man's saying Simon is the best guy ever he's ever met, and he's a really nice bloke, and Simon wears great shirts and . . .' It got a laugh, which diffused the tension while I worked out what to do next. Another time my laptop crashed and it took 35 minutes to get it going again. I took questions from the audience and did a live business surgery while I waited for the tech guys to resurrect my laptop.

Learn your way around the control panels for your chosen presentation software (normally Keynote or Powerpoint). Some people use split screens on their laptop, for example, and you need to check that what you are seeing on your screen is what the audience is seeing on the overhead screen – or it can be embarrassing!

Use props. I present some 'bitesize' talks to give an introduction to my business courses, and at these I sometimes give out newspapers to teach people how to find business ideas by looking for trends, successful company reports, big adverts and so on. This can be an icebreaker too and a great way to 'show, not tell'.

Don't forget your work/life balance and don't be lured by the glamorous appeal of a far-flung speaking gig. Ask yourself, is it worth travelling a long distance or being away from home for a significant amount of time to attend or deliver a talk? Can you afford the time away from running your day-to-day business? What about the costs involved? Can you maximise your time and expenditure by getting a holiday or mini-break out of the trip?

Learn to say no. Business can be addictive and it can be hard to turn down a moneymaking opportunity, but sometimes it's the right thing to do.

Go to Interpreneur.com/resources to get extra materials and free Internet Marketing training

CASE STUDY

Stas Prokofiev

wifiwealth.co.uk

I have tried my hand at many different courses and so-called 'gurus' who all promised that I will be able to make money online, but unfortunately none of them ever gave any results. Once I spent £600 to launch a product online which made me just £7!

By this stage I was frustrated and ready to give up the online business idea. Then I found a set of DVDs I had bought at an entrepreneurs bootcamp several years ago. Simon Coulson was one of the speakers at this event and he really stood out to me, as he seemed like a normal, genuine guy who had made millions online and was sharing his story and strategies.

After watching him on DVD I felt really inspired and excited about making money online again. Shortly after this, I decided that I would go on Simon's 3-day Internet Marketing Diploma course. I attended the course in June 2014 and at the time I was working as a shift manager at an airport.

The *Internet Business School* course completely changed my life. I learnt so much and was now confident that I could make money online by applying the knowledge Simon gave me. Within just three weeks I had built my own website and 3-4 weeks later I was making money online, working for local businesses, handling their online marketing affairs, building more websites and making videos. This continued to grow and I was able to make thousands of pounds in the coming months, all thanks to Simon's course and all generated from my home in west London.

What made this course different to any others is that it was very clear and informative, it gave me confidence to really understand how the tech side works, and most importantly I was left with a clear action plan of what I needed to do to be successful. In short, the course made me take action and see results faster then anything else I have tried before.

My earnings have grown massively and I am now able to generate more in a few hours per month on a part-time basis than I got working 45+ hours a week to earn in my old job at the airport.

Since gaining the skills in Internet marketing I have also got involved with running my own events and showing others how to build their own online businesses from scratch. So far my best day has made me £2k!

This has changed my life in a huge way, and I am now able to afford things I would have taken months or even years to save for before. I have been able to have several nice holidays with my wife and finally I have the chance to buy myself the new BMW convertible I have always wanted.

I'm still hungry for more success - I am only 27 - and want to achieve a lot more in the online marketing world. Without the help of Simon and the *Internet Business School* I would not be where I am today. I thoroughly recommend it to anyone, and as long as you take action you will definitely see great results.

CHAPTER 15

Rolling The Dice, Again

Another new business came to me via a friend called Alan Bell. Alan had seen me speak at a seminar around 2008 and lived locally, so he made an appointment to see me. He wanted to talk about a joint venture on a product he had created, which was aimed at helping over-50s to start a business.

Some months after this joint venture discussion Alan got in touch again. This time he had a new business proposition he had been working on with a friend called Mark Jones. Mark had worked for some top-tier football clubs such as Coventry and Athens as a commercial manager, and he'd also held senior positions at some of the country's best known racecourses too.

Mark had seen that football clubs sometimes had their own private club lotteries that allowed supporters to win cash prizes and support the club at the same time. Typically these kinds of fundraisers were run in a very old-fashioned way, with money collected in buckets and paper tickets handed out. In fact, Mark knew of one club that had done away with its lottery because it was so outdated and not profitable for the club. In that case the lottery ticket sellers were each given a free season ticket in exchange for selling tickets and collecting money each week. The chairman had decided he could make more money from simply selling the season tickets he was giving away and so he scrapped the lottery.

However, Mark had an idea to change the model of how these lotteries worked. He identified that the problem lay in the collecting of the money, however the National Lottery had come along and shown us that money could be collected online instead of in a bucket – genius! Clearly, if sports clubs sold their own lottery tickets online they could replicate some of the success of the National Lottery for their own means.

It was a great plan and if we got Premiership clubs on board we anticipated we could make a lot of money. I sat down with Mark and Alan and between us we came up with a model to sell to clubs. We decided we'd set the online lottery up for clubs for no upfront fee and with a £50,000 prize, while for their part the club had to promote it; over their public address (PA) system, in match programmes and on banners and leaflets. They would also have to add to the prizes by offering things like dinner with the team or the chance to watch a game from the dugout.

I'd never done anything like this before and I was so busy with *Internet Business School* and my information product empire that I certainly didn't need it, but I was excited by the idea and I embraced the challenge of doing something completely different. I'm the sort of person who gets easily bored and so I'm always willing to explore new avenues, and this one was certainly new territory to me. I believe that dreams can't be too big – and the fact this might have been 'out of my league' did not put me off at all.

We got a software designer to build us a website where you could buy lottery tickets by direct debit. It was a 'cookie cutter' type of website which would basically enable us to customise the site for individual clubs by using the same template but changing the name and logo and so on.

We also needed a licence from the Gambling Commission, this involved all three of us getting vetted in a process that took about six months! Then we needed to find a company that printed cheques. Who printed cheques? I had to turn to Google to find the answer to that question, then that was another box ticked.

Finally it was time to sell the idea to clubs, and the three of us put our best suits on and pitched up to a string of clubs, including Chelsea, West Ham and various county cricket and rugby teams. Walking into Chelsea was another one of those surreal moments. Here I was, an average Joe, pitching to a Premiership club!

Ultimately we didn't get Chelsea's business as the club had sold its media rights to third parties which threw a spanner in the works, but we did get West Ham and plenty of larger football teams, rugby teams and county cricket teams too. I was involved in this business for about 18 months, and it was a very exciting rollercoaster of a journey. We made a profit once it was up and running, but ultimately it wasn't as profitable for me as my own businesses, because the lottery tickets only sold for £2 each and of course all the money we made was split three ways.

I decided to quit while I was ahead. I'd loved the excitement of being involved with Premiership clubs and I enjoyed learning about a totally new industry, but when I looked at the hours I put in compared to the return I was getting I had to concede that my time would be better spent on my own businesses, so we agreed to sell the business to another larger lottery provider. This was really how I learned the lesson I mentioned earlier, about thinking carefully about joint ventures. Don't be too quick to get involved – however dazzling the opportunity sounds!

This is probably a good place to mention another thing you should be wary of, in terms of using your time wisely. As your business grows, don't be afraid to delegate the admin and necessary accounting and bookkeeping you have to do. I used to do my own VAT returns every three months (you currently have to register for VAT when your turnover tops £83,000 a year) and I absolutely HATED it. I found it stressful and boring, and I'd lock myself in a room and force myself to do it, resenting every minute.

After about a year of torturing myself like that I hired outsourcers to do this for me. Bookkeepers cost about £15 an hour, so it really was a false economy for me to sweat over the books and VAT returns myself. Nowadays I put all my receipts in a box and give them to my bookkeeper. All my income is on my bank statements, so I hand those over too. It's easy – and far less stressful than doing this myself.

Having said this, don't over-delegate. There are some jobs that you can do yourself very quickly and easily. For example, incorporating a company is one of the things you can quickly and easily do for yourself, so there is no need to pay an accountant or 'formation agent' to do this for you. To incorporate a company nowadays is very simple - you just go online to Companies House and follow the easy instructions.

This is also a good point to mention another 'gamble' I took – and in this case it was a gamble that didn't pay off, twice!

When speed dating first became popular several of my friends tried it. I listened to their stories and their strategies – they all had different ways of approaching it and varying degrees of success – and I decided to put together a guide on speed dating. It seemed like a great subject for an information product. I knew anecdotally there was a hungry market out there, and after checking out the interest and competition using Google Trends and looking at the number of Google adverts that popped up when I searched for 'speed dating guide' and the like, I was satisfied nobody else had written a similar guide, and I was confident it would sell.

I hired an outsourcer to compile the guide as a downloadable ebook, put together a website and waited for the sales to take off. Then I waited, and waited, and waited some more! The ebook was priced at £20 so I dropped the price a bit, but still only a handful of customers bought the guide. I then lowered the price to £10 and got a few more sales, then £5 and got several more customers – though at that price my profit margin was so low it was questionable whether I'd actually make any money.

After that I decided to test something out. I put the ebook on sale for free in exchange for a name and email address, so at least, if nothing else, I would get a mailing list out of this, thinking I could work out what to do with the list if the speed dating guide really did crash and burn. Guess what? As soon as I made it free 100 + people downloaded the ebook. What this told me was the market was there but the potential customers didn't want to PAY for it. That was a big problem, and it was an important lesson to learn. In some markets there can be high demand and low competition, but there isn't the propensity or willingness for customers to get their wallets out.

The 'willingness to get the wallet out' factor can be driven by a number of things. In the case of speed dating, people may have thought they could get this information for free if they just looked hard enough online. After all, it sounds a lot easier to find and decipher information on speed dating than to plough through say, the Land Registration Act 2002, to work out how to claim abandoned land and property, doesn't it?

They may also have decided that it only cost about £10 to go on a speed dating night, so why not just do it and find out all about it that way? They probably thought that could be a better investment.

It was a lesson, but it didn't crush my dreams of making money from the dating game, oh no! Using the mailing list I'd amassed and my experience of membership sites, I later started my own dating website. I put up about 20 profiles of friends and acquaintances who gamely agreed to give it a go and I did some Internet marketing to encourage other people to post up their profile for free. I got about 300 people this way, at which point I decided I'd reached a 'critical mass' and could now start charging £4.95 a month for membership.

People did sign up, but not in anything like the numbers I needed to make this a success. I realised how woefully inadequate my database of daters was when I got an irate message from a guy in Inverness complaining the nearest potential date on the site lived 123 miles away from him! I had to admit defeat – you literally need tens of thousands of profiles for a dating site and I think I'd lost interest by that point. I'm sure if I'd have persisted I could have been bigger than Tinder . . . honest! Instead I decided to cut my small losses and concentrate on matching myself up to a more profitable venture.

LESSON TIME! Simon Says:

Think carefully about joint ventures. Is the percentage profit a good enough split? Is it worth your while getting involved or would you be better off pursuing another venture on your own and taking ALL the profits?

Go to Interpreneur.com/resources to get extra materials and free Internet Marketing training

Don't be too quick to get involved with opportunities, however exciting and glamorous they seem, and know when to quit when you're ahead.

Delegate administration chores and bookkeeping – your time is probably far better spent on growing the business, not getting bogged down with boring chores. That said, be careful what you pay for. Some things – like incorporating a company – are free and easy to do yourself.

Xero.com is a useful Cloud-based accounting system if you do want to do your accounts yourself.

Always consider the 'willingness to get the wallet out' factor when deciding what to sell. You might have found a hungry market with no competition, but are people WILLING to hand over cash for your product?

If your customers can find the information you are selling for FREE and they can do this EASILY – or they think they can – you have a problem. All the information in my original Bulgaria property guide was free, but the key factor was that it was TIME-CONSUMING to find it, and TIME IS MONEY.

CASE STUDY

Jamie Davies

bristolbusinessconsultants.co.uk

I'd been interested in Internet marketing for years but it was seeing Simon speak at the Entrepreneurs Bootcamp in Brighton in June 2015 that really gave me the kick-start I needed.

At the time I was working as a recruitment contracts manager and my days never really ended. I use to wake up at 4.30 a.m., travel and spend 10 hours working, then after returning home I would still be dealing with calls and emails. I wanted to change my life and find a way of making some decent money that didn't involve such long, uninspiring hours.

From all the speakers at the 3-day event Simon stood out to me. He seemed like a normal, down to earth guy. I spoke with him briefly and that's when I knew I had to do something. I was approaching 30 and it felt like the time was right.

I decided to do the *Internet Business School*'s Internet Marketing Diploma in October 2015 through the distance learning package, preferring to go at my own pace. I chose the Diploma as I thought that if nothing else, at least I'd have a qualification that could help me get another job.

From day one of starting the course and watching the videos I was hooked. It was very informative and gave a plain step-by-step system of putting everything it taught me into place. This gave me the confidence to understand how even the 'tech' side worked, something that had held me back previously.

Just being able to set up a website was worth the investment of the course. I had been trying out a few things such as affiliate marketing and selling information products in my spare time, but it was very hit and miss. After completing the course I was able to change a few things and it really took off. I then completed other courses with the *Internet Business School,* some included within the Diploma package. One was the Local Business Marketing course, and that really gave me the springboard I needed.

Armed with the know-how and confidence I got from my courses I tested the water by offering my services as a local business marketing consultant in Bristol, where I am based. This went well and I ran a small business in my own time around my job. From this I was able to leave my job in June 2016 and start my own business full-time, while at the same time completing more of Simon's courses, such as Affiliate Marketing, Outsourcing and Business Accelerator.

One of the important strategies I learned was to test pricing, and to understand that lowering your price isn't always the best option. I had been selling an information product on eBay for £5 that wasn't doing very well. There were a few similar products around the same price so I worked out how I could squeeze my costs and lowered the item to £2.50, again only selling a couple. From the tips Simon gave I changed the title and increased my price to £7 – then I sold 10 in the next two days. Sales were very good from then on and so I tested pushing the price up further to £9, and I sold over 100 copies. I built my own website, then a number of others, and everything I needed to know had been shown to me through the *Internet Business School* courses.

My earnings have grown from hardly anything to monthly recurring revenue of around £2,000, which only takes a few hours a month of maintenance to sustain. This allows me to work on growing the business with other products, including working on joint venture projects with other companies.

My lifestyle has changed completely now I am working for myself. I have been able to upgrade my car and take mini breaks that I wasn't able to do before, but the greatest luxury is freedom and being able to choose which work you want to do and having the option to say no. I'm so glad I took action and chose Simon as the man to help me. It's the smartest business move I could have made.

CHAPTER 16

Don't Buy A Porsche!

Early on in my journey, as I've already mentioned, I'd bought myself a Porsche as this was my dream car. However, as I've also admitted, I sold it after a year. I'd hardly used it. The reality was it was actually quite uncomfortable to drive, there was no space in the boot for a suitcase or shopping, and because it was a bit of a special car I was worried about leaving it in certain areas. In addition, my friends had done nothing but ridicule me about it being a 'hairdresser's car', on account of the fact it was bright yellow.

Despite knowing all about my experience, Rick (the fireman and drummer, who I had mentored to start his own business, How2Become), also dreamed of owning a Porsche. Despite me advising him that in my experience this was vanity over sanity he still went ahead and bought one. I wasn't really surprised when he too found that he hardly drove it, and just like me, Rick sold his 'dream' Porsche after a year.

I thought it was a lesson that could be useful to others, and so I began to work this story into my presentations when I spoke at entrepreneur seminars. I had an accompanying slide titled 'Don't buy a Porsche', warning entrepreneurs that buying any super flash sports car like that was just an act of vanity, and that in my view there was in fact no point in buying one. After all, the attendees I was addressing were in the business of MAKING money not wasting it, so I questioned why would they want to spend thousands on a car that was, in my opinion, more ornament than use. That was my message, and I delivered it over and over again, cautioning anyone who would listen to stay clear of posh sports cars.

However, at this point in my story I have to hold my hands up and admit that, ultimately, vanity triumphed over sanity once again. You'd have thought I'd have learned my lesson but, on no, I hadn't!

It was now 2011 and I'd hit another million pounds in sales. I happened to notice a gorgeous Ferrari for sale in a car showroom window. I had a little voice in my head warning me not to give in to this shiny attraction, but I couldn't help it. I told myself that I had now got to the point where I could afford to have a Ferrari, and a bright red one at that, so why not just buy one? I could afford it, so why not?

I told a few friends I was thinking about getting a Ferrari and they all quickly reminded of my Porsche experience and indeed my advice to others about not buying silly cars.

Did I listen? Well, I tried. Partly to appease my friends and partly because I was really trying not to do anything daft, I thought I'd hire a Ferrari for a weekend just to see what it was really like to drive. I thought that was a really good way of finding out if I could REALLY see myself owning one. So, I did just that and hired one, putting it to the test and driving it all around Kent for a couple of days. What did I think? Honestly, I have to say I hated it! So, I added this experience to my Porsche advice in my on stage presentation, with a follow-up slide saying 'don't buy a Ferrari either!'. The advice was based on the following observations I had made after my test weekend. In my opinion:

1   Ferraris are incredibly uncomfortable to drive. They are designed for smooth racetracks, not potholed UK roads, and as such the rock- hard suspension literally jars your spine with each little bump in the road.

2   It's impossible to listen to a stereo or hold a conversation whilst the engine is running. The reason for this is there is a glass panel behind the driver's head that lets you see the engine. It's a nice idea, but this also means there is an awful lot of cabin noise from that engine which renders the radio useless and any conversation with other passengers impossible.

3   Whilst driving around in a Ferrari, particularly in an area where the sight of one is rare, you are greeted with what I called the 'Ferrari hello'. This comes in two varieties: the first is from Ferrari appreciators and is a bib of the horn, a thumbs up or a wave; the second is a certain other, derogatory hand gesture which is not so polite and leaves you feeling somewhat deflated when it happens.

4   Ferraris do less than ten miles to the gallon if you use the right-most pedal at all.

5   The biggest problem is that, wherever you go, people STARE. If you enjoy attention you might like that, but personally I prefer to be somewhat more anonymous. In a seminar I told a story about one time when I was getting petrol and noticed the entire queue was staring out at my Ferrari. Even funnier was the fact the cashier was just staring at the car too – hence the long queue! Red traffic lights became the bane of my life, because when you are sitting at the lights in a Ferrari people in neighbouring cars bend over to peer through the windows of your car to see who is in it. They imagine it may be someone incredibly famous, then give a look of disappointment when they see a face they don't recognise! Letting people down like this does nothing for your self-esteem, I can tell you.

I recounted all this advice, concluding in a very clear 'Don't Buy A Ferrari' message when I spoke to nearly 8,000 people at the Entrepreneur's Bootcamp in 2009 at the London O2 Arena.

Imagine my concern, some weeks later, when a letter arrived on the doormat with the Ferrari logo on the envelope. My heart almost stopped when I saw this, as I feared it was going to be from Ferrari's legal team about my defamation of their brand on stage. After all I had very publicly dissed them at one of the largest arenas in Europe!

When I opened the letter I was relieved to see that it wasn't a legal letter at all, but rather an invitation for me to try out the new Ferrari California model at the Millbrook test track in Bedfordshire for a whole day for FREE. It was a bit like a 'Red Letter Days' type experience but for no charge. Irresistible? Indeed it was, and so I went along just thinking to myself it would be a fun day out for nothing.

However, there are no prizes for guessing what happened next. Yes, that's right: when I saw the Ferrari California I fell in love! This new model addressed several of the shortcomings of my earlier Ferrari experience. Firstly, this was the first ever Ferrari with an engine under the bonnet and not behind the driver's head. This meant the cabin noise was significantly reduced and you could both enjoy the stereo and hold a conversation in the car. Further, the suspension could be changed at the flick of a switch on the steering wheel, from a comfortable setting for UK roads to a hard setting for the racetrack.

I came away from the track day persuaded that I needed one of these, and as the California was a new model this meant there was no option of going for a second-hand car – it would mean buying a brand new Ferrari! The list price was £143,000… and that was before I got to any upsells.

I decided I ought to justify this kind of expenditure by turning it into a business opportunity too. I knew that there was such a long waiting list for Ferraris that a second-hand one could sell for more than a brand new one, as often it was the only way you could get your hands on one. Therefore I figured I'd sell it for more than I'd paid once I'd got bored, and I also decided I'd hire it out for weddings. I'd seen other businesses doing supercar hire and I figured this could be an enjoyable business. I could use the car myself but also hire it out, so I'd effectively get paid to own a Ferrari! With this in mind I registered a domain name for the website for *ferrarihirekent.co.uk*.

I placed my order and went into the dealers to 'spec' out my car. Here I witnessed a masterclass in upselling, which is well worth sharing, and indeed I have done many times in seminars since.

This is how it went. First I had to choose the trim and options for the car. I chose black as I thought this would be more incognito and I really hadn't enjoyed all the attention I had got when I hired the red Ferrari. Next I had to choose the wheels. The standard wheels were a nice, 5-spoke alloy and I told the dealer I'd take the standard ones. He pulled a face and said, 'Sir, no one has ordered the 'standard' wheels from here'. I felt like some real cheapskate and felt compelled to look at the 'optional' wheels, choosing some others that weren't that much different, but added nearly £3,000 to the bill (to be honest

I preferred the standard ones, but the shame of feeling like I was cheap made me upgrade).

We all experience this kind of upsell all the time, being made to think the standard model is somehow inadequate when compared with the 'professional' edition, or the 'platinum version'. The salesman then asked me which steering wheel I required. I looked at the two options in the brochure and genuinely couldn't see any difference at all. He went on to explain the 'option' wheel had embedded LED lights that would light up when I needed to change gear, a technology developed for Formula One. The Ferrari California was the first ever production car to offer it, but I questioned if this was necessary as the car was automatic! The salesman politely explained that if I put the car in manual mode I could change gears with paddles on the steering column and then the lights would help me know when to change gear. I was still unconvinced so I declined the upsell. The dealer then pointed that EVERY California they had sold had taken this option, and if I chose not to take it then my car's value in the resale market would be severely affected. So, I took this upsell too! This pattern was repeated for a couple of hours and I ended up committing to over £29,000 of upsells.

I got to take the Ferrari out on a track day at Silverstone and had the time of my life. We were free to race against other Ferrari drivers out on the track day too. It's about as close as I'll ever get to the boyhood dream of being a racing driver!

Check out the pictures on the photo pages!

Everyday use of the Ferrari was not such fun. Whilst it was more practical than the Porsche in some respects, it was such an expensive car I was scared to take it anywhere. In car parks I became paranoid of someone knocking the doors and I wouldn't leave the car anywhere dark at night in case somebody decided to sabotage it out of spite or malice. I didn't even use it to visit friends unless I could park on their drive away from public view, and most of my friends simply didn't have houses like that!

I got a puncture one day and tried to get a new tyre. No one in the UK had one, not even Ferrari, as the particular specification of tyre from Pirelli I needed was so new to the market. The only place to get the tyre was from the Ferrari production line in Italy, so my new tyre had to be flown in at a cost of almost £1,000 – the most expensive flat tyre ever!

So, after a year or so, history repeated itself and I sold the car. My business hopes didn't really work out (I think people prefer old classic cars to Ferraris on their wedding day). I worked out that for the amount I used it, it had cost me around £12 per mile covered! I probably shouldn't have done that calculation, should I?

Anyhow, it was certainly one to tick off the bucket list, and I don't have regrets. I have great memories of buying the car and racing it around a Formula One track at full speed, and they are memories you really can't put a price on. At least it had a good resale value and I didn't have to take it to a car brokers at the end of the day (see Garry Steele's case study at the end of this chapter!).

LESSON TIME! Simon Says:

Don't buy a Porsche!

Don't buy a Ferrari!

In fact, don't let VANITY beat SANITY in ANY of your purchases! I am not saying don't have fun, but in my experience you'd be better off hiring a swanky car for a holiday or a weekend, say, but then sticking to a more practical motor for everyday use. That way you'll have the best of both worlds – and you won't pay £12 a mile for the privilege! Today I drive a BMW i8 – an electric hybrid that does over 40 miles to the gallon and has supercar looks and performance.

CASE STUDY

Garry Steele

autocarbrokers.co.uk

Whilst running my own consulting business back in the mid-noughties I was keen to see how I could branch out into the Internet world and use this medium more effectively for some business ideas I had.

I had always wanted to deal in cars in one way or another, but for most people who like the idea of doing this there are always two key things that hold them back. First, it's money, because buying cars with which to trade is not cheap. The second issue is space, because you need somewhere to store these cars.

And that's where 'Car Broking' came into being! It completely solves these two problems, because as a broker you never actually own the cars or have to store them – in fact you rarely even see them. Whilst I built this business up, I could begin to see how others could use my knowledge and expertise as a real business opportunity, and as a result I created a comprehensive business guide called *'How To Become A Successful Car Broker'*. This contains everything you need to know about setting yourself up with a business that you can run from home, part-time or full-time, with minimal start-up investment.

However, I also knew that I had to use the Internet as a means to reach a much larger audience with this opportunity. Enter Simon Coulson, who I met when I attended one of his first seminar events in Bournemouth back in 2007. Simon showed me how to use the power of the Internet and what I would need to do to put his online business concepts into practice. It was Simon's positive 'can-do' attitude that helped me find a way to take my business forward, thanks to doing his course I was able to set up my website, *autocarbrokers.co.uk*.

How has this been received? Well, over £500K in sales demonstrates the success of my business – which is something that anyone else can enjoy as well... and not many businesses operate on a 90% gross profit margin!

The initial and continued success of my business has helped me in so many ways, and not just in fringe benefits like holidays, but more importantly it has provided investment for my other business ideas. I am enjoying running the business and looking for new ways to expand. This is another thing I learned from Simon: it's all about developing multiple streams of income. I'm 63 now and all of this I have done from my home in Taunton, Somerset - thus keeping my overheads extremely low. I'm very glad I met Simon because without his advice and guidance I would certainly have struggled and no doubt lost a lot of money, so I remain extremely grateful.

CHAPTER 17

Tasting The
High Life

Having said everything I have about owning the Ferrari, I must admit that this was not my only flashy indulgence. Before I REALLY learned the lesson about not letting vanity win over sanity, I tried all kinds of other swanky things in my misguided quest to live the high life. I learnt quite a lot along the way, so I think it's worth sharing some of my experiences and lessons learned.

Let's start with my trip to the British Grand Prix in 2010. Standard day tickets cost about £300 and when I was working for BT I could never afford to go. Things were different now, so I decided to have a proper VIP day out and treat some business contacts and customers, including Andrew Reynolds, to thank him for the speaking gigs he'd got for me, plus my mate from the band, Rick.

I heard that getting into Silverstone was a nightmare in terms of traffic. I had some business to do beforehand so I was concerned about how I would manage to get there on time. As a result I decided to check out if I could travel by helicopter.

I called up a helicopter hire firm that did a shuttle service into Silverstone and asked if they could take four members of my group of about 10 or 12 who were going to travel this way. The company was able to do it, so the next task was to work out where we would be picked up from. The helicopter firm suggested a small airport and a hotel both local to me in Kent, but when they named the hotel I was confused.

'I know that hotel and it doesn't have a helicopter landing pad.'

'No, but it has enough space in its grounds for us to land.'

I looked out of the window of The Great Barn at the several acres of grounds surrounding me, and I had a better idea.

'Do you think you could pick me up from home?'

After a quick check on a map the helicopter company told me that was no problem at all.

'Do you want me to mow a 'H' in the grass or anything?'

'No, that's not necessary, but you can if you like!'

I actually did, just for the fun of it! And when we took off I gave a jokey royal wave to the neighbours who came out to see what was going on.

It was pretty special arriving at the Grand Prix by helicopter. Just seeing how other people reacted was quite a laugh and I certainly felt like a VIP. I'd bought us all the grandstand tickets and we got to meet some of the drivers in the pit lane and had a silver service dinner made up of loads of courses.

Meeting the drivers was a great experience and I loved having my photo taken with the race winner that day, Mark Webber - you can see the photo in the picture section. Unfortunately the food was a bit posh for my taste and at one point I sneaked off and grabbed a burger from a van! I have to say it was delicious, and I enjoyed it far more than the fancy food served by the glitzy silver service VIP catering.

Getting home by helicopter was also something of a let-down – almost quite literally! For a start the traffic wasn't even bad enough for us to justify the helicopter, and then on the way back a warning light came on in the control panel. The pilot started looking in his instruction booklet to find out what it meant, at which point Rick turned white and started saying 'let's just land and get a taxi'.

I was less concerned – as a natural optimist I just don't see the world in terms of what can go wrong, only what can go right.

'It'll be fine!' I said. 'Don't panic! I'm sure it's nothing to worry about!'

Moments after I said this the pilot decided he had better call out a replacement helicopter, and we landed as quickly as possible. Then we had to wait for the replacement helicopter to take us home, which meant we didn't even get back home any quicker than we would have done by road!

In total I'd spent several thousand pounds for the day out. Was it worth it? Yes, because I have no regrets. It was a memorable experience, it was important to treat my business associates and all the guys had thoroughly enjoyed it (even Rick, once he'd got his colour back!) I wouldn't repeat it though, because the VIP elements just weren't worth the extra money and we'd have had just as good a time with the standard tickets, a burger and a car ride there and back.

After that I had another experience that didn't really live up to expectations. I've been a Sting fan for years, and when I saw that he was playing an intimate gig for just 200 people in London I went on eBay and bid for some tickets. They were a few hundred pounds each, but that was as cheap as I could get them, and I figured it was a once in a lifetime chance to see him in such an intimate setting. Unfortunately, when I arrived at the venue – St Luke's Chapel – it was clear Sting wasn't going to be belting out Police hits like *'Walking On The Moon'* or *'Message In A Bottle'* as I'd imagined. He was in fact sharing the stage with a famous lute player, and he was singing old English folk tunes along to the lute music. It was random and unexpected, and clearly a pet project for Sting. Oh dear!

Fortunately, that is not my only experience of seeing Sting. Before this I'd had a much better experience when I saw him play in Monte Carlo. I took my partner at the time and we flew in a helicopter across the sea from Nice to arrive in Monaco and stayed at the famous Hotel de Paris, which was spectacular. The concert was brilliant too. It was a small black-tie affair (with no lutes!) and neither were there any warning lights on the helicopter – a triumph!

Despite enjoying the Hotel de Paris and other luxuries from time to time, this was not a world I had grown up in or was accustomed to. It meant that I often relied on the general reputation of places when I was deciding where to stay, or where to go on holiday. Most of my good friends didn't have the money for swanky 5-star trips and so I had no word-of-mouth recommendations to go on. Monaco had definitely lived up to its glamorous reputation because the setting of the hotel was amazing. However I made a mistake when I decided to go on holiday to Barbados…

In my mind Barbados would be the most idyllic Caribbean island destination you could ever imagine. I mean, if it was good enough for Simon Cowell, it was good enough for me, right? Unfortunately, the reality was I found it underwhelming.

Of course the sand was white and beautiful, the sea was a stunning turquoise blue, but I'm not the sort of person who's content to lie on a beach for a fortnight and I found the island too small, too flat and too boring. The nightlife - or the 'strip' as it was ambitiously called - consisted of little more than a few tin sheds, something I found disappointing to say the least!

I'd seen the whole island in a day and ended up taking a plane to neighbouring St Vincent for a trip, just for something to do. Now that really was magical – the tropical wonderland I'd expected Barbados to be, complete with waterfalls and stunning coastlines. It just goes to show the generally accepted image and reputation of a place doesn't always give you a true or accurate picture of what it is REALLY like. Now I'm more cautious about visiting so-called 'must see' destinations. They are only 'must-see' if YOU want to see them!

Las Vegas was another place I'd heard great things about and had high expectations of, but I think you can probably already guess where I'm going with this! It seemed that it simply HAD to be on your bucket list and of course it is a destination favoured by many of the world's rich and famous. What could go wrong? I expected it to be absolutely incredible – a thrilling, once-in-a-lifetime trip - but again I can't say I was overly impressed.

I'm not a gambler, so the casinos weren't a particularly exciting attraction for me. I saw Elton John play in his Red Piano tour which was pretty cool, I also saw the famous Cirque de Soleil but was it worth flying across the world for? If I'm totally honest, not really. Once again I'd bought into what I imagined I ought to be buying into now I had plenty of money to spend and could afford to live like the rich and famous celebrities who made places like this their haunts.

Another thing that happens when you become successful and wealthy is that you get invited to all kinds of swanky functions that are not necessarily your thing. One of these was at the Dorchester Hotel in 2010, and it was a charity ball I was asked to attend by one of the seminar promoters I'd worked with. Posh balls have never appealed to me, but I've learned there is a sense of obligation when you're invited to something like this. It's polite to attend and it's good for business, as you need to keep your contacts happy, and the fact it's for charity means you really don't want to say no.

I dutifully bought the penguin suit and a pair of new shoes and went along to support the event. Just like at the Grand Prix, I was faced with course after course of fancy food that was a bit wasted on my simple taste buds, and then it came to the charity auction. This was of course the main reason I was invited along, as after being wined and dined by my hosts I was expected to bid in the auction, like all the other wealthy, invited guests. I can't remember what I won now, but I know I spend a few grand, and I also politely bought a set of raffle tickets at £50 each! I didn't mind at all as it was all for charity, but it was another eye-opener for me about status and money, and what happens when your successful reputation spreads.

After making a donation to the Make-A-Wish Foundation I was asked to attend various other balls and events, and I did my best to go along whenever I could and bid in the auctions. This is a charity I really support, as it grants wishes and provides holidays for sick children with life-threatening illnesses, and I was very happy to do my bit.

One prize that caught my eye was the chance to have dinner with the 'dragons' from the TV show *Dragons' Den*. For an Interpreneur like me, this was an irresistible opportunity and I bid £5,000 to secure my place around the dinner table, along with five dragons and four other winning guests. I really looked forward to it and wondered if I might pick up any good business tips or advice.

It turned out to be an interesting evening. One of the dragons, who shall remain nameless, was over an hour late and then was the first to leave, so that was quite an eye-opener! The conversation flowed quite well, though I felt most of the dragons kept their guard up and remained very true to their TV persona. Deborah Meaden was the exception. She was nothing like the character we see on TV. She wasn't scary or dragon-like in any way – in fact she was absolutely lovely. Unfortunately I can't say I picked up any business gems but I did enjoy myself and I love being able to say I've had dinner with the dragons!

At another charity event I bid for VIP tickets to see Coldplay at the O2. Being a massive Coldplay fan and of course being in the tribute band, this was something I was prepared to splash out on, and happily I won the bid. I decided I'd treat the guys in the band and I think I paid about £2,000 in total for us all to go to the concert and have backstage passes.

The concert was absolutely brilliant, but imagine our disappointment when we went backstage at the end . . . only to find that Coldplay had left the building! Of course, when I looked at the VIP tickets I'd won in the auction they didn't actually say we'd definitely MEET the band, but that was certainly our expectation and we'd fully expected to see them in the backstage bar after the gig. Another lesson learned!

It seems, perhaps, that fate was trying to tell me something when it came to meeting Coldplay, because I had another disappointment ahead of me. There was a competition on the radio to win a pair of tickets to a Coldplay gig in Germany. Included in the prize was the chance to travel by private jet to the event with the band. The radio station wanted to award the tickets to the biggest Coldplay fan in the country, and so you had to answer a load of questions and sing a Coldplay song to progress through the competition. To my delight I made the final two (I told you I was a massive fan!) and was invited into the radio station for the grand final. When I was standing in reception I met the other finalist.

'Shall we take each other?' he asked. 'That way whichever of us wins, we'll both get to go to the gig.'

It was a good idea as the prize was a pair of tickets, but this presented me with a moral dilemma: I'd promised Dan, our bass player in the band, that I would take him if I won the two tickets.

'Let me text my friend,' I said. 'I need to run this past him.'

I texted Dan but got no reply, so I told the other guy I'd better not take him up on his offer as if I won it wouldn't be fair on my friend. Needless to say, I was then hoping like mad that I would win both tickets and could take Dan. Unfortunately, I didn't win, and when I came out of the studio afterwards my phone beeped. It was a text from Dan saying: 'Yes mate, go for it!' Arghhhh!

Now, I certainly don't want to come across as being ungrateful about any of the experiences I've had since starting my million-pound businesses. I know I am in a very fortunate position, and the only reason I have shared some of the stories about the 'downfalls' of having money is that I want to stop YOU from making mistakes with your hard-earned cash.

Having money is actually brilliant, and being able to share money around through supporting charities and treating your friends and loved ones is something you should value. It's something you can't put a price on, and knowing there is more to life than just money is crucial to your happiness. Money CAN'T buy happiness – but it can help in many ways.

I was reading my emails one day when a very exciting request popped up in my inbox.

'Would you be interested in taking part in Channel 4's *The Secret Millionaire*?

'Yes!' I thought instantly. 'What a fantastic opportunity!'

If you don't know the television programme it follows millionare benefactors as they leave behind their day-to-day life and go undercover in deprived areas to find out who needs their help. This was something that really appealed to me and I was very keen to take part and immediately started thinking up ideas about who I would like to help and how.

Channel 4 sent a camera crew to my house for an initial shoot, and it was only then that I discovered the dates they needed me were just impossible to do.

'Is there any way we can work around this?' I asked.

Unfortunately the TV schedule and mine just couldn't tally, and in the end I had to forgo my chance of being a 'secret millionaire.' Maybe I'll get another chance in the future. I hope so, because one of the most valuable things about money is being able to do stuff like this and help other people.

LESSON TIME! Simon Says:

Don't be flash for the sake of being flash. Find out exactly what your super deluxe, gold-plated VIP pass or ticket is going to give you. Sometimes being segregated in a VIP area is actually LESS fun that being part of the main crowd so do your homework before you part with your cash.

Personally, having experienced the high life in the past I have to say I'm much happier with steak and chips than a six-course meal, and in jeans and a tee shirt rather than a penguin suit. We're bought up with these stereotypes of a successful lifestyle, but make your own mind up and ask yourself *is this really for me?* I know it isn't for me. I haven't been in a helicopter for five years and my holiday is one cruise a year, but that is how I like it.

Just because a holiday destination, event or attraction has a 'must-see' reputation, check out if it's really going to live up to your expectations. Don't rely on glossy images in magazines or folklore. Instead, talk to people who have actually visited these places and check out online reviews.

Give to charity but don't be afraid to say no, and don't feel obliged to go to every event. Choose causes close to your heart and be in control of how much you give and how you get involved. Giving is also gift to YOU so don't let it become a drain. Enjoy it and remember that giving your time is also a gift.

CASE STUDY

Guy Cohen

www.ovitraders.com

I was fortunate to have a private introduction to Simon and I immediately saw that I could benefit from his practical business experience and vision. I had already developed stock and options trading platforms for my own private use, and I was at the point of offering licenses to individuals to help pay for the research and development I needed to move my venture to the next level.

I did an Internet Business School course in 2009, when I was in my late 30s, and Simon quickly identified that in order to survive, let alone maintain the required research and development to turn this into a profitable business, I would have to treat the software development side of things as a business in its own right.

Simon explained that in taking a more commercial approach my customers and I would all get what we wanted: a suite of world class trading applications for our own investments. Keeping the customers happy would mean they would keep renewing and extending their memberships to my site, which would bring money into the business for research, development and growth.

To this end, Simon advised that we would need to expand to offer customers more products, ranging from ebooks, entry level applications, a monthly subscription model, live workshops all over the world, webinars and so on.

This was a daunting prospect and my fear was that it would restrict my personal trading but I need not have worried as, with Simon's help, I got the balance right.

Each new product I offered was useful and was a reasonably priced stepping-stone on a high quality trading journey. This resulted in an extraordinary proportion of my students remaining with me for years and achieving extremely impressive trading results.

Go to Interpreneur.com/resources to get extra materials and free Internet Marketing training

Before I met Simon I looked for investment from joint venture partners and affiliates, but Simon had the foresight to know that we would not be able to rely on these forever and that we would have to develop our own ability to generate leads.

The overall result is that I've been able to not only produce outstanding trading applications for my own use, but have become commercial without alienating a wonderfully loyal customer base. In fact, my students have become even more loyal, which is extremely unusual in my industry.

The business has comfortably turned over £1 million + per annum for several years now and is poised for significant growth, and this is without external investors or loans. This is no mean feat, especially as I have achieved all this with a very small team.

I'm delighted that I have been able to turn what was effectively a software hobby into a truly global business, while also enjoying the perks of such progress. Travelling to exotic destinations to hold our events has been one such perk, and I am very happy working between bases in Surrey and the US.

It has been enlightening to be able to create world class products for my own use, while also learning business skills, running the software development as a business, maintaining customer loyalty, and turning consistent profits at the same time. The combination of all these has also led to sustainable product development and profits from multiple streams.

I could not have achieved this without Simon. He is a real person with real success, and his magic dust has transformed my project into a sustainable global business.

Anyone who is serious about their business should get as much time as they can with Simon and the Internet Business School. The magic happens when you embrace the lessons and go the extra mile to apply them.

CHAPTER 18

Learning From
The Best

You might be wondering what pressing engagement I had that was so immovable I couldn't shift it to accommodate Channel 4's *The Secret Millionaire.* Well, when I explain what it was I think you'll fully understand why I couldn't just rearrange my diary at the drop of a hat.

The reason I couldn't do the TV show was because I was about to travel to Necker Island, to spend a week in the company of none other than the king of entrepreneurs, SIR RICHARD BRANSON! I also had a string of other business commitments in the diary, some of which had already been shuffled to enable me to take this trip of a lifetime – so becoming a secret TV star unfortunately had to go on ice.

I came to have this amazing opportunity to go to Necker through a guy I met in London and in the States, who was on the entrepreneur's speaking circuit I was now a fully-fledged member of. He told me that, once a year, he hires Necker Island for a full week and invites a few selected '7-figure entrepreneurs' to join him. Then he asked me if I would like to be one of these very privileged guests. YES was the answer – and I think it took me less than a nano-second to give it!

He explained the idea was that each invited guest would pay $40,000 for the privilege of being in this 'mastermind group'. There would be business sessions each day during which the group would mastermind each other's businesses throughout, sharing our secrets of success in different industries and seeing how we might help each other out. In addition we'd all agree to give a day of our time to Sir Richard's charity foundation, Virgin Unite, which unites entrepreneurs with people from all walks of life, to help improve lives around the world. In return we'd get to hang out with Sir Richard and each spend at least one meal each day with him, as well as with each other. It sounded absolutely brilliant and I couldn't wait – and I think you'll be pleased to hear that on this occasion I definitely wasn't disappointed with my trip!

I started planning my travel straightaway, and it's just as well I did because it was quite a logistical feat to get to Necker. For a start I phoned Virgin Airlines – who else? – only to discover they couldn't fly me there! 'But I'm going to your boss's house! You have to be able to get me there!' I wanted to cry, although of course I didn't.

I discovered I needed to take a total of seven flights that would get me as far as Tortola, a neighbouring island with the closest airport to Necker. From there I could take a boat or a helicopter for the final leg of my journey. Now, I hadn't had the best experience of helicopters following my day at the Grand Prix, but things had gone well in the South of France when I went to the Sting gig. All things considered I figured that had to be THE way to arrive on Necker, and that no doubt all the other multi-millionaire guests would take this option too.

Things did not go to plan. My luggage didn't make the first transfer, which meant it was six flights behind me, and so when I finally arrived on Tortola I only had the clothes I was standing up in. I went shopping to kit myself out but could only find tourist clothes with 'Tortola' emblazoned across them. This meant that when I landed on Necker I was like a walking advert for Tortola – and to add to my embarrassment I discovered all the other entrepreneurs had decided to arrive by boat. What a prat!

Anyhow, my humiliation was soon forgotten. I'd seen Necker on TV and it was as magical as I expected it to be. Sir Richard's grand house sits on the top of the hill and has huge doors that fold out wide so you can look at the spectacular views and scenery all around. The beaches, the lush vegetation, the pink flamingos and the giant tortoises – everything is perfect, and you really feel like you are in paradise.

Sir Richard was exactly as I expected him to be – refreshingly down to earth, polite, and a person who clearly has good values. He joined us every day, was very free with his advice for us, and he even took us out on his catamaran and arranged for a visit to the neighbouring island he had recently purchased too.

There was no side to him at all – he made us all feel very welcome and was generous with his time.

In one of our mastermind sessions we asked Sir Richard what his best pieces of advice were. He didn't hesitate in telling us that we should hire the best people, have fun and make our business a happy place to work. It sounds so simple, but this philosophy has clearly worked incredibly well for Sir Richard. I remember his advice every day, and I'm grateful to my mum as she instilled those values in me as a child too. We had a fridge magnet that said 'It's nice to be important but it's more important to be nice' and I've never forgotten that.

I asked Sir Richard where he gets ideas from for all his different companies, and he said a lot of his ideas have come from a bad experience. A good example of this is when he launched Virgin Airlines. He'd had some bad experiences on long-haul flights and thought how he could improve the customer experience – and this is how he came to put video screens in the back of the seats. I was really interested to hear this and it reminded me of my air-conditioning venture, which came about because I couldn't get the service I wanted from air-conditioner sellers who were already in business.

It was very interesting to meet the other guests too – they did everything from being a golf pro who ran a huge golf-training site to operating airport security systems. I also picked up some good tips from them and, to my surprise one guy told me his best advice was to fire his customers.

'FIRE customers?' I said, incredulous. This definitely didn't sound happy, fun or nice!

'Yep, just sack them, get rid of them. All the ones you don't want – give them refunds and send them packing. Work with better people!'

This entrepreneur was in the coaching field, and he explained that he had found it a soul-destroying experience to attempt to coach customers who were not sufficiently engaged to ultimately stand on their own feet and make a success of their business. His advice was

My villa in Spain

Me at my holiday home in Spain, on one of the most expensive holidays I have ever had!

A helicopter landing in my back garden

Just landed at the British Grand Prix

Me at the end of the pit lane at the British Grand Prix

Me and Mark Webber; the race winner

The Ferrari California I purchased brand new

Taking the Ferrari around Silverstone 2011

Helicopter to Necker Island from Tortola 2011

Coming in to land on Necker Island

An inspirational week on Necker Island with Sir Richard Branson

Heading out with Sir Richard to board Necker Belle

On board Necker Belle and golf buggy fun on Necker Island - do you drive on the left or the right?

My most prestigious gig ever, performing on Necker Island

At Virgin Radio, about to miss out on a private jet trip with Coldplay to Germany

Visiting Ferrari World whilst speaking in the UAE, 2013

Speaking alongside Sir Richard Branson, Anthony Robbins and Lord Alan Sugar, not a bad speaking booking for the reluctant public speaker

Me and Tony Robbins

Meeting Chelsea Clinton after speaking alongside her dad, Bill Clinton, at the London Excel Entrepreneurs event, 2012

Speaking at the Entrepreneurs Event at the London Excel Centre, 2012

On the same bill as former president Bill Clinton

Go to Interpreneur.com/resources to get extra materials and free Internet Marketing training

The Internet Business School team photo, 2014

Delivering training for the Internet Business School

Teaching in Slovenia, as the Internet Business School goes global!

Meeting Baroness Michelle Mone OBE, after speaking alongside her at an event in 2014

Speaking at the London Excel Centre, 2012

Laptop lifestyle on a safari after teaching in Johannesburg , 2014

On stage delivering our Diploma program, 2015

Exhibiting at the Business Show 2016

Speaking at the O2 Arena, 2009

Performing with the band at the O2, 2009

Go to Interpreneur.com/resources to get extra materials and free Internet Marketing training

Dream property comes up for sale

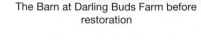

The Barn at Darling Buds Farm before restoration

Work underway to restore the Barn

The Cart Lodge needs a little bit of work

Restoring the Farmhouse

The stunning Barn taking shape

The new roof to the Cart Lodge going on

Me and Philip Franks (Charley from Darling Buds of May) when he visited the farm

The Farmhouse at Darling Buds Farm

Me and my latest Border Collie, Zeta

The Barn is all restored! - Alongside
me is Barney

Me being interviewed for ITV's
'This Morning' show

Darling Buds Farm is open for business!

The classic car show in my back garden

Proper country gent, outside the Larkins
Farmhouse

Me outside the Oast House at Darling
Buds Farm

Aerial shot of Darling Buds Farm before I restored it, July 2002

Aerial photo of Darling Buds Farm, post restoration

Go to Interpreneur.com/resources to get extra materials and free Internet Marketing training

Clubdraw customer - West Ham's website

The Songwriting Academy, 2014

Me and Martin Sutton, co-founders
of The Songwriting Academy

Songwriting Academy Workshop,
2015

In the Rutherford's studio for The
Songwriting Academy music production
course - where The Living Years amongst
many others weres recorded

One of the many successful
Songwriting Academy
retreats held in Spain, 2016

Working in the studio on my next
composition

Red carpet invite to a film preview!

Me in a rare photo with all 3 Border Collies; Amy, Zeta and Barney

Me on a cruise in the Carribean

Go to Interpreneur.com/resources to get extra materials and free Internet Marketing training

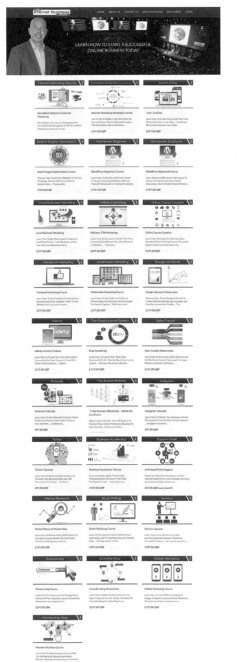

An Internet Business School Diploma course,
being filmed to reach larger online audiences

Business owners learning how to grow
their businessesonline with the
Internet Business School

Me teaching at an Internet Business School
Internet Marketing Diploma course

The Internet Business School range of
courses continues to grow, 2016

The Great British Business Show
at London Olympia

Go to Interpreneur.com/resources to get extra materials and free Internet Marketing training

On stage speaking at Brighton Centre 2016, 13 years after seeing Coldplay perform on the very same stage that was the catalyst for this whole journey

Standing ovation at Brighton Centre

to put up prices so you get a better quality of customer – the type who are as committed and enthusiastic to their project as you are.

I've since followed this advice and I have found it beneficial – I hadn't even realised how draining it was to work with demotivated people. As an aside to this, there is something else I want to say about having your energy drained. I've found out the hard way that if a customer asks for a refund – in your opinion unfairly – then you should not deal with this yourself. It's completely demoralising when you believe this person is just pulling a fast one or trying to rip you off and not pay for the service you have provided. Always get someone else to process the refund if it reaches this point, as doing it yourself will just create NEGATIVE ENERGY - energy that you simply don't need.

Another guy I met on Necker ran a carpet cleaning business, and one night over dinner I plucked up the courage to ask him how he managed to make millions from a business that essentially cleaned carpets for about $200 a time and employed only three members of staff. His answer was surprising but simple: this entrepreneur didn't actually make his millions from physically cleaning carpets, but by doing about ten seminars a year, teaching people in that industry about how to get clients and how to make money from carpet cleaning.

Later in 2011 I was lucky enough to share a stage with Sir Richard when we were both speakers at the same conference – the National Achievers Congress at ExCel London. Sir Richard was a guest speaker along with the self-development guru Tony Robbins and Lord Alan Sugar. We were all asked to talk about the specific strategies used to make our businesses a success, and when it was my turn to talk I also told the audience I'd decided to conduct a little social experiment.

My experiment went like this. I asked the audience who they thought was the best speaker at the conference. Was it Sir Richard? When I put this to the crowd of about 7000, lots of people clapped and cheered. Next I asked if Tony Robbins was the most popular speaker there. Tony's fans were a bit more rah-rah and razzmatazz and started punching the air and giving each other high fives. Lord Sugar's fan club was not quite as forthcoming when I called out his name – only about three people piped up!

Anyhow, continuing with my little experiment, I told the audience I was going to go on Google and see what the answer was when I typed in 'best speaker at ExCel'.

Lo and behold, the name Simon Coulson popped up in 7 of the top 10 positions on Google. I then explained how I'd created a brand new website the day before and made a video at the venue and got that on the first page too. My lesson, of course, was that you need to know how search engines work to harness the full power of the Internet and make your own brand and business stand out on Google. I think this went down quite well, judging by the crowd's appreciative reaction.

The following year, in 2012, I appeared on the same stage as former US President Bill Clinton, when we both spoke at the 'Entrepreneurs 2012' conference at London's ExCel. I was on before him and there were Secret Service agents all around, which was pretty different to any talks I'd given before! About a year after that, I attended a cocktail reception and gala dinner hosted by the Clintons at the Guildhall, in aid of the Clinton Foundation. Bill Clinton was in attendance and James Blunt gave a private performance, and I was lucky enough to chat to Chelsea Clinton and have a photograph with her – she was very charming and I got a great snap for my Facebook page!

Success certainly breeds success, because then I received an email from Oxford University inviting me to speak to its MBA students. I had to look twice at the request and the name of the prestigious institution. I blinked, and my very first thought was 'Do they have any idea I went to a once OFSTED-failing comprehensive school?'

Once I knew this was for real, I must admit my immediate reaction was to feel slightly nervous about the invitation, as this was something very different to my usual speaking gigs. The number of people I'd be talking to would be far less than I was used to addressing at venues like the ExCel, so that wasn't an issue. What made my pulse race was the somewhat surreal scenario of me, Simon Coulson, an ordinary bloke with mediocre exam results that would certainly not have got me into a top university, addressing some of the world's finest business students.

Of course, I didn't let my nerves stop me from accepting this invitation – it was another opportunity of a lifetime and I grasped it. The talk I prepared was similar to the speeches I gave at all the seminars and workshops I did, but without making a pitch or selling anything at the end. This meant that I was in the position where, once again, I was telling myself that this was no different to anything I'd done before.

Walking into the historic, landscaped grounds of Oxford University was still quite a moment to savour. I'd seen the prestigious 'dreaming spires' on television and in photographs, but stepping foot inside the campus was really something special. The vibe was like nothing I'd experienced before, and being amongst the bustle of students at one of the oldest universities in the world was, well, not at all like walking around the streets of Gravesend!

I gave my talk in the Nelson Mandela Lecture Theatre and as planned I did what I'd done many times before. It went pretty well, although there was one awkward moment when I talked about my student who had founded her very successful permanent make-up business after I mentored her. By way of explaining to the uninitiated what permanent make-up actually was I described how you could have your eyebrows tattooed, for example, so you didn't have to apply eyebrow pencil every day. My mistake was to address the men in the audience when I was giving this explanation, as typically I've found in the past it's the men who are not familiar with the concept of permanent make-up. However, one of the students pulled me up on this and accused me of being sexist, and I had to hold my hands up and admit this had not been a very politically correct move on my part. Lesson learned! I should have altered my style to better suit the audience.

LESSON TIME! Simon Says:

Learn from the best. Do the best courses and attend the best seminars you can afford, given by speakers with a proven track record.

Keep listening to advice, keep asking questions and never get complacent. You never know what you might learn that may help you improve your business.

I once heard someone say in a seminar 'If you want to be rich, copy a rich bloke' - a good bit of advice. I think my mastermind trip to Necker, although expensive, has paid great dividends from the lessons learned from the other 'rich blokes' there - including Sir Richard himself.

Consider your audience, or whomever it is you are selling to. Think about whether you need to change your style to fit your target market, no matter how successful your formula has been in the past.

CASE STUDY

Izzy Arrieta

littleredhorse.co.uk

I heard Simon speak in November 2013 and attended the 3-day course in January 2014. At the age of 40, this gave me a complete mind and skill shift. I was buzzing for the whole of those three days, and filled with an exciting sense of opportunity.

I'd worked in the media for many years and had a great career, but I was constantly away from home, putting in incredibly long hours and, after nearly 20 years, I wanted to try something new. My whole life has been about communication but until I heard Simon speak I didn't realise how incredibly exciting I found the web. For instance, I had not heard of affiliate marketing or indeed many of the other ways to have a business.

When Simon mentioned Local Business Marketing I really wanted to do that, helping local business owners through offering great websites and videos. I love telling the stories of others and giving people a voice. You can do that through TV and radio, or in print, and you can also do that online. After years of frustration and not knowing what to do with the next stage of my life, I suddenly had something to be excited about! Not only that, it was something that would use my existing skills in journalism and producing/directing, and it was something I could do no matter where I was, all I had to do was get online.

I built a website for my partner, who's a builder, which immediately brought results as he became much, much busier. I also built a few more sites for friends and hosted them to cut my teeth before taking on paying clients. I soon dumped having a boss and we have since moved from Leeds to a lovely home we are renovating in Cumbria.

I love being able to suggest ways forward for business owners who have got a bit 'stuck', and to share the knowledge I have. For instance, to be able to produce a Facebook advert that will reach thousands of people for £20 is amazing!

My Internet business earnings have boomed and my partner's business is flying too. Best of all, life is less stressful. I love being my own boss and I don't have to leave my dogs every morning and go off to make someone else rich, not knowing when I will return!

The Internet has changed everything for me, and for a relatively low investment it's incredible how you really can propel you and your business forward like never before. I truly am living the dream right now, and discovering *Internet Business School* was absolutely life-changing.

CHAPTER 19

Living The Dream

Remember I said that when I bought my house, The Great Barn, it was only half a mile from the farm that was used as the set for TV's *The Darling Buds of May*? Living deep in the Kentish country, so close to this idyllic setting, had been a huge part of the attraction of The Great Barn for me. There had been many times when I'd really felt like I was enjoying the life of my childhood dreams, living in a rural country house with a river running beside it and being king of my castle, just like Pop Larkin was king of his manor in *The Darling Buds of May.*

Of course, The Great Barn wasn't really a match for the large, ramshackle Larkin estate, which included a farmhouse, an oast house, a Tudor barn and a cart lodge, set in 35 acres of land. My place had about three acres of land around it and was in an idyllic setting too, but it was very modern by comparison. I'd refurbished the barn to a really high spec, something I'd devoted a lot of time and money to over the years, and it was not really the sort of place the Larkins would have been at home in. Nevertheless I'd have LOVED to swap places and own old 'Buss Farm', which was the real name of the farm hired out every year by Yorkshire TV, when they filmed the series in the early 90s. Oh yes, I'd have traded my luxury home for the dilapidated old farm in the blink of an eye, because owning that estate was the ultimate dream for me.

Imagine how I felt when I heard, back in 2012, that Buss Farm was actually up for sale, and at a price I could afford. It had been in the same family for many, many years, and from snippets of information I'd heard over the years I could not have imagined the family would ever sell up. They had even been reluctant to let Yorkshire Television film there when they were first approached by producers who told them it was the ideal place to bring *The Darling Buds of May* - an adaptation of H. E. Bates' 1958 novel – back to life.

My heart honestly nearly skipped a beat when I heard it was for sale. Owning it would be a magical, and I immediately looked into buying it. It was on the market for £1.35 million and I estimated it needed a lot more spending on it, as it had fallen in to a state of disrepair over the years.

Viewing it was very exciting, even though I could see there was an incredible amount of work to do. As I looked around I had flashbacks to scenes of the smiling Larkin family feasting on a big roast chicken, laid out on a groaning table in the garden in front of the oast house. I could picture Catherine Zeta-Jones' Mariette marrying her Charley, played by Philip Franks, and the pair of them running through the idyllic English countryside surrounding the farm. Funnily enough, Charley had been like me once upon a time – a wage slave trapped in a soul-destroying office job, working as a tax inspector. He too had a wake-up call that prompted him to transform his life – in his case this was seeing how Mariette and her family lived the rural idyll, not falling down an escalator like I had!

I didn't need to imagine the soundtrack of the TV show as I viewed the property, as there were birds singing, geese honking and animals mewing in neighbouring fields. Right from the moment I stepped foot inside Buss Farm I felt very strongly there had been a missed opportunity to capitalise on its TV history, and it was in a such dilapidated state that I felt quite sorry for the old place. I'd seen the farm on my telly week after week in the early 90s as I sat with my granny, basking in the Larkin family's warm glow. This was a golden opportunity, and I was completely sold. It really was my childhood dream come true, and I was already making plans in my head about how I could restore the farm to its former glory, and preserve and cherish its status as a national TV treasure.

So, I made an offer below the asking price. I was in a strong financial position, not needing to sell my previous home, and happily my offer was accepted and I got to buy my ultimate dream property. News that I'd bought Buss Farm quickly spread around the neighbourhood, not least because I agreed to give interviews to the local press to talk about my plans. I explained that I'd taken the farm on as a project and not just as a home, and that I'd applied for planning permission to revamp, rebuild and convert the farm buildings into my rural dream.

I didn't need all the space to myself, so I'd decided to renovate three of the farm buildings into guesthouses offering 'perfick' holiday accommodation, and to completely refurbish the main Grade II listed farmhouse. I figured there would be lots of Darling Buds of May fans who would love to come on holiday to the farm. I'd change the name too, to Darling Buds Farm. What else?

It took a year to get all the necessary planning permission. This was partly because of the listed status of the farmhouse, partly because there were some rare protected species of creatures living in the surrounding countryside, and partly because 100 people objected to my plans. Many of them thought, I was trying to create some kind of tacky theme park, which taught me a lesson about communication - talking to the local press about my plans to pay homage the *The Darling Buds of May* was perhaps not the best idea, as some of the articles didn't explain my plans in the kind of detail I'd have liked.

Anyhow, building work started in January 2014. I employed 20 builders on the site for a year and the first building was open in July 2014, the next in September 2014 and the third in April 2015. As well as doing holiday lets I decided to apply for a wedding licence, which came through in the summer of 2016. You can now hire the whole 12-bedroom site for a wedding, plus there's extra accommodation available in glamping-style shepherds' huts in the grounds. The marriage ceremony room is in the Tudor barn, which is over 300 years old, and it's spectacular. Brides-to-be gasp when they walk in because you could not ask for a more idyllic setting. The room is lined with timber beams and gives spectacular views across the duck ponds, stream, cherry orchard and ancient woodland. There's a wooden wedding gazebo in the grounds too, so you can have your photos taken surrounded by Kentish countryside. If you want to find out more, take a look at the website: *darlingbudsfarm.co.uk*.

I'm absolutely delighted with what I've achieved, and visitors keep telling me I've done an incredible job. The work isn't quite finished yet as I'm still improving the grounds and collecting more vintage farm stuff to give it the Larkin feel! I have an office at the farm and am living there with my three Collie dogs – yes, I even got to make my Enid Blyton dreams come true! It really is a little corner of paradise and I count my lucky stars every day. Have a look at the before and after pictures in the photo section, and if you ever need a place to stay in Kent then check us out!

LESSON TIME! Simon Says:

Believe that dreams can come true, because if they can for me, they can for YOU.

Be careful what you say. In talking to the press I created problems for myself and raised concerns about my plans unnecessarily. CARELESS TALK COSTS TIME AND MONEY!

Posing with a big grin on your face in the local paper can also rub people up the wrong way. I experienced some problems created by jealousy that threatened to hold up the building work at one point and that did cost me money. All in all, best to keep your mouth shut until you unveil your finished work!

Don't forget the value of outsourcers as you expand your business and make lifestyle changes – I have used outsourcers from many fields in the creation of the farm.

CASE STUDY

Dirk Van Loon

dirkvanloon.com

I was already working as a business consultant but after 10 years I felt I needed an injection of energy and to sharpen my skills and focus. Part of my business is about teaching others how to expand creativity in order to boost their business success. I had reached a point where I personally needed inspiration from elsewhere, which Simon was able to provide.

I live in Belgium and I did an online course from the *Internet Business School*, when I was approaching 40. The most helpful parts for me were learning about outsourcing and online marketing. My revenue increased by 50% and my book, *The Secrets of Influence: Mastering the Art of Inspirational Leadership,* became a number one international bestseller on Amazon.

The entry level of the *Internet Business School* course is very affordable and gives you a good basis from which to move to the next level afterwards. I'll most likely do more courses in future, but for the time being I am very happy with my business. I can do what I want, when I want, and I am able to develop and share my experiences. *Internet Business School* was definitely money well spent.

CHAPTER 20

Passion Projects

I've always been a fan of Howard Jones, and at one of his gigs he did an acoustic number and told the audience: 'I wrote this on a songwriting retreat in a chateau in France'. My ears pricked up and not just because I was enjoying the music. The idea of a going on a songwriting retreat really appealed to me. I'd crafted a few tracks over the years and had really enjoyed creating 'Make It Happen' when I played with the band at the O2, but I still had a lot to learn - and let's face it, if Howard Jones could benefit from a songwriting retreat, I certainly could!

It was 2013 and I was looking at having a holiday, so I got to thinking that I could take myself off on a songwriting retreat like Howard Jones, and make that my holiday. I could think of nothing more relaxing and enjoyable than tinkering away on the keyboard, learning and improving my craft and hopefully soaking up a bit of sun or enjoying exploring a new place at the same time. As I've said before, I get bored easily, and even on holiday I like to have interesting things to do, so this seemed a perfect scenario for me.

I did a bit of hunting around on Google to see what was out there in terms of songwriting retreats and a name popped up that rang a bell – Martin Sutton. I then remembered that someone at a seminar had once told me about a guy who ran retreats for musicians - I think it must have been after I'd told the story of performing 'Make It Happen' at the O2. I didn't act on the information at the time, but a songwriting retreat was clearly an idea that appealed to me, as I hadn't forgotten the name.

I found out through the Internet that Martin was a full-time songwriter and ran retreats from a villa in Spain, so I contacted him and booked myself in for a stay. I couldn't wait. I was sure it would be a great experience, and even if I didn't come up with the next number one record I was fairly confident it would be a great break – certainly more enjoyable than revisiting a villa in Murcia, I reckoned!

There were about a dozen other people on the retreat and when I arrived I immediately thought to myself 'why have I never done this before?' I do like holidays, but I've struggled over the years to find trips and packages that suit me – Barbados is another case in point. This was different. I absolutely LOVED it from the minute I arrived until the minute I left.

The songwriting itself was really enjoyable and it was great to be actually learning the craft properly instead of busking it on the keyboards and teaching myself as I'd done for years. I also loved the conversation by the pool, working in a pleasant climate and playing back what I'd achieved that day over a glass of sangria as the Spanish sun set over the hills.

I liked it so much I went back in 2014, and this time I asked Martin if he had thought of expanding the business.

'It's such a fantastic experience,' I said, 'and I don't think a lot of people know you can even do something like this.' (I know, I was meant to be on holiday, enjoying some leisure time, but once an Interpreneur, always an Interpreneur… and remember what I said about ALWAYS keeping your eyes and ears open for business opportunities?)

Martin was interested to hear what I had to say, and I explained that I could see there was potential for him to take his business to a much wider audience using the Internet to market it. He actually had a lot of hit records under his belt, but relatively few people knew about him, the retreats and what they could gain from going on one.

Martin and I arranged to meet up in the UK a few months later, when we bounced a lot of ideas off each other. The upshot was that we decided to start a new company that we would co-own. Martin had the industry contacts and experience of running songwriting courses and he would be the lead teacher, while I had the marketing skills to really help the business grow and reach more customers.

We called our new enterprise *The Songwriting Academy (thesongwritingacademy.co.uk)* and as well as offering lessons in songwriting we decided to provide coaching on music production and useful business skills. For example, teaching students how to self-publish and release their music on Spotify and iTunes, plus how to make demos. record and produce music, and how to deal with royalties. We put together a range of different courses, chose dates and venues and then put the whole lot onto a new website.

To launch the new business we did a preview event in London and we also invited award-winning teachers to come in. Martin had an impressive contacts book which included people like Rob Davis, who co-wrote Kylie Minogue's multi-Ivor Novello award winner 'Can't Get You Out of My Head'. Rob joined us as a songwriting/production consultant, along with a long list of other well established, highly respected music industry moguls, like Cliff Masterson who is a composer, arranger and producer and has worked with artists like Little Mix, Emeli Sandé, Lionel Richie and Kylie.

Bringing in industry experts was priceless, and not just in terms of giving students the best teachers. In the music industry it's all about who you know, so by bringing in these fantastic contacts we could offer our students access to people who could potentially help them fast-track their careers, if they had ambitions to go to the next level.

We held the first weekend course on the Darling Buds Farm – the perfect setting for a retreat - and it went really well for the students as well as for me, as I took part and had a great time. If I'm honest it's not the most profitable business I've ever set up, but to be involved in an industry I love so much is absolutely priceless. I feel very lucky to be able to call this work. It's great to inspire and encourage new songwriters AND it does return a small profit for everyone involved, so what more could I ask for?

It's amazing what happens when you plug in some online marketing to an expert in an industry. We're now training over a thousand songwriters a year with industry professionals and this year we've run 3 x 7-day songwriting retreats in Spain for 40 people each time. We've given up-and-coming songwriters the chance to learn and co-write with Ivor Novello award-winning songwriters with over 200 million record sales between them. We're currently in talks to expand into the USA and Australia and we've also launched an unsigned songwriter competition and have had over 1000 entries in our first year. In addition we have secured partnerships with Caffe Nero and Yamaha music, and all the proceeds have gone to Stand Up For Cancer and Nordoff Robbins, the leading independent music therapy charity in the UK.

This brings me on to another 'passion project' I'm happily involved with. When I bought Darling Buds Farm I inherited a classic car show event with the property. For 20 years the previous owners of the farm had kindly allowed a local car club to use the grounds for their annual classic car show, and everyone involved hoped that I, as the new landowner, would keep this tradition going. Living so locally and being a car enthusiast I'd actually attended the car show in the past and really enjoyed it, so I didn't hesitate in agreeing to keep the show on the farm.

In fact, it was when I'd visited the car show a few years earlier that I'd first learned that *Darling Buds of May* fans used to turn up at the gate, hoping to be able to look around. In those days they were very often turned away, and I remembered this when the farm came up for sale. To me it seemed such a shame to deny fans the chance to see a piece of TV history, and that's how I started to dream about paying homage to the farm's TV history and welcoming Darling Buds fans in.

Anyhow, I was delighted to inherit the car show and I saw it as an opportunity rather than an obligation. I've always loved cars, and how could I resist the chance to host a classic car show in my own back yard? It was another boyhood dream come true really. The event is also a charity fundraiser and this appealed to me too. It was a great chance to give something back and so I threw myself into it.

First I had a look at what had been raised in the past and how, and then I had a think about how I could improve the event for all concerned – visitors, exhibitors and ultimately the recipients of the charity money. The most obvious thing I could bring to the party was to use my Internet marketing skills to get more people to come along, support the event and ultimately boost the charity coffers.

I discovered that in its previous 16-year history, in total the car show had raised something in the region of £100,000, but I was confident I could get more people through the door and improve on the average annual sum raised. I had 35 acres of land which meant there was plenty of space to accommodate more visitors, and so I set about doing publicity in the local press, and online, including promoting the show on Facebook.

Of course, the more visitors we had the more staff we'd need, but I wanted to keep outgoings as low as possible. With this in mind I did a deal with the event staff agency that would provide workers for the show. In return for them providing 12 staff I offered to give the owner of the business a free *Internet Business School* course. In addition to this I asked for students and coaches from *Internet Business School* to volunteer their services, inviting them all to stay on the farm the night before, when I'd put on a barbecue, a bit of a party and some live music. This worked a treat – I got lots of help without it costing the charity pot any money, and it turned the job into a fun weekend break for everyone. Crucially, I got motivated staff who had were all very engaged with the event, and there was a positive 'can-do' vibe amongst the whole team when we opened our doors to the public.

The event was a huge success with thousands of people attending and it has got better every year. In the four years I've been in charge the show has raised tens of thousands of pounds for local charities. The show has also grown to become one of Kent's most popular annual summer events, and this year we had more than 900 classic cars and over 60 stalls selling burgers, beer, local jams and fudges and all sorts of other local produce and crafts. *The car show is at the start of July; if you want to come or volunteer to help out you can find out more info at darlingbudsfarm.co.uk.*

On the day of my first show I looked around and couldn't believe how lucky I was to have all this in my back garden. We had Pop Larkin's yellow Rolls Royce (of course we did!), plus vintage American Corvettes, old ambulances and police cars, all kinds of old charabancs and cars from the 70s and 80s. We also had all sorts of entertainment, like a Punch and Judy stall, Supercar display, Morris dancers, a vintage fair and traditional rides for the children. It was hard work and I was running around like a headless chicken with a Walkie-Talkie and an earpiece in, trying to coordinate things, but it was brilliant. When we handed over the cheques to Kent Air Ambulance and Demelza House Children's Hospice it was the icing on the cake – I honestly felt as proud of that as I did when I made my first million. You could say that's when I really, truly knew I'd made it.

LESSON TIME! Simon Says:

Remember what your mother taught you? If you don't ask you don't get! I had nothing to lose when approaching Martin Sutton about going into business, even though I had no idea how he would respond. Look what we have created!

Think about your hobbies – is the thing you love something a lot of other people love too? If it is, can you turn your hobby into a business or a sideline?

Whatever life throws at you, look for the OPPORTUNITY within. There is always one there. To date I have built five 7-figure online businesses that between them have generated more than £20 million in sales – and the first £2 million was from my spare room, fresh from quitting my job.

Be kind. Be generous. Give your time. Create opportunities for others. Celebrate your success and smile.

CASE STUDY

Paul Gillon

Websites4startups.co.uk

When I turned 30 I decided I wanted to change my life. I was working in a gym in Scotland at the time as I'd just moved there and I've always enjoyed fitness, but it wasn't what I wanted to do for the rest of my days.

I wanted to do website and marketing work from home, working for myself. My aim was to be able to work from anywhere in the world. I was inspired to do this because my girlfriend at the time had been given the opportunity to take her work to Barbados and I wanted a job that would give me the freedom to do the same, if I wanted to.

This was how I came to take the plunge and go on Simon's intensive 3-day Local Business Marketing Course. I spoke with my parents and they were very supportive and loaned me the money to visit London and take the course in 2012.

There was a lot to take in at first so I gave myself a fairly steady start when I launched my business. Slowly but surely the hurdles and challenges that presented themselves to me were quickly solved when I remembered all the things I had learned from Simon's course, and I was able to tackle them head on. I started my first website within a week and started learning more and more as I continued down the path of becoming a website developer and marketing consultant. It is now five years down the line and I have over 70 clients, many new friends in business and my work has taken me to places like Portugal, Tenerife and all around the UK.

Through being a local website and marketing consultant and developer my work and success has caught the attention of many. We have been featured in local newspapers and social media blogs and have built up a very good name for ourselves. Through my work I have recently been lucky enough to meet celebrities such as; Joe Calzaghe, Paul Gascoigne, Ricky Hatton and Bret 'The Hitman' Hart.

I am now earning as much as £8k some months which is a lot more than I used to earn in my old job! While the money I earn is great the best thing about what I do is the freedom. Now I work with my partner and we enjoy being able to pick and choose how we spend our time. We have a baby on the way and so we are planning to take a month off to adapt to having a new member of the family. Being able to do that is priceless and we can do this because when we work we work hard. Furthermore we continue to develop our skill sets and bounce ideas off of each other on a daily basis.

Future aspirations include taking on more family members as staff who we truly trust, as sometimes it feels like we have discovered a secret! It's amazing where this journey has taken us, and it's all stemmed from that decision to go it alone after doing Simon's course. I've since taken additional courses, and I'm always happy to fund them and take what I need from them to further my business.

Taking the *Internet Business School* course was the catalyst that has now helped me create the lifestyle I wanted. I enjoy my work with a passion, and I have no boss and no commuting in the morning. It's not an easy route – you have to work very hard and be motivated – but it's definitely worth making the effort for.

INTERNET BUSINESS SCHOOL FAQs

I'm asked all the time about *Internet Business School,* so here's what I say to the FAQs.

Q. Is it as important as you say to use the Internet for business?

A. Yes, 100% crucial! The Internet has become the number one source for clients of businesses. It outstrips all other channels such as television, newspapers, directories, referrals and radio. It's essential for ANY business owner to understand how to leverage the power of the billions of online customers around the world.

Q. How do you teach students at *Internet Business School*?

A. There is a wide range of classroom-based training courses, and online digital home study programmes. I also offer 1:1 personal coaching, a mentoring programme and a variety of 1-day workshops.

Q. Who are your typical students?

A. There is NO typical student! The school attracts people of all ages across all levels in business around the world, from beginners who are just starting an online or offline business, through to existing business owners who either don't have a presence online or want to improve what they currently have. Some are thinking of quitting their job, newly redundant or fresh out of school, college or university. Many are looking for a career change or wanting to generate a second income, and some are returning to work after taking time off to have children or care for family members.

Q. Which is the most popular course?

A. The intensive 3-day Internet marketing course - the Diploma in Internet Marketing. This teaches all the important concepts of Internet marketing online, the essentials for creating a website, the multiple ways to drive traffic to your website and how to convert traffic into sales and profit. It includes how to sell to website visitors, how to build a recurring income, how to keep your customers coming back time after time, how to provide content, how to sell other peoples' products, how to build a relationship so your customers trust you, and how to make sure a customer becomes a lifetime customer and not just a one-off.

Q. Why is the Diploma so popular?

A. My students have literally created MILLIONS online. The course is also great value for money as it incorporates lots of smaller courses that you can do separately if you wish, but are included in the Diploma package for no extra cost. These include *'How To Create And Sell Online Courses'*, *'How To Write And Publish Your Own Book or eBook'*, *'How To Become A Local Marketing Consultant'*, *'How To Make Money With Affiliate Marketing'*, *'Outsourcing Course'* and the *'1,000 Resale Rights Library'*.

Q. Do you get a qualification if you study at *Internet Business School*?

A. Yes! *Internet Business School* has been accredited by NCFE (*ncfe. org.uk*) as a Diploma-awarding body in Internet marketing and by CPD, the Certification Service (*cpduk.co.uk*).

CASE STUDY

Julia Haydon

WordPresscourseslondon.co.uk

Ever since I can remember I've always been really passionate about business. I loved the thought of taking an idea and creating something from it. I spent several years in the military as an aircraft engineer and had a couple of great jobs, but I could never get away from that feeling of being frustrated by company hierarchy and the lack of control I had over certain aspects of my life. Whilst I was getting paid what most would class as a good salary, I remember feeling something was missing.

In March 2012 I accidentally walked into a seminar talk called Business 2012 at the O2, which was being given by Simon. I remember being excited by what I'd learnt from just one hour of listening to him. My friends were a little sceptical, but I decided to book onto Simon's weekend course nonetheless.

I never thought buying a 3-day course would have had such a huge impact on my life. I had studied at university for three years but what I came away with from three days was so much more valuable in the 'real world'. The skills I learnt from Simon not only enabled me to create websites and get them ranking in top position on the first page of Google, but he showed me how to get tasks completed in areas where I didn't necessarily have the skill set, and so much more. When I purchased the course I remember thinking that it was expensive, by the end of the weekend I thought what amazing value it was as I had learnt so much.

The day after the course I started putting into practice what I'd learnt. At the end of the first week I had built a website, had a new logo and flyers designed. I had accomplished so much – I couldn't believe it!

Within months of building my website it was ranking on the first page of Google. It now ranks at 'Position 1' on the first page of Google and other search engines. I offer WordPress training courses around the country and abroad and I'm delighted to have worked with; Hitachi, Duke of Edinburgh Awards, University College London, King's College London, Sutton Council, Croydon Council, Medway Council, Visit Kent, Chamber of Commerce, universities, schools, colleges, start-ups and many more. The company goes from strength to strength. What I was earning in a year is now what I earn in only a few weeks of working part-time, when I want to work. My best month ever was £15,500 – amazing!

The journey has been fantastic. At the age of 39 I'm now starting the next business from my base in Surrey. The opportunities really are endless. Simon is one of the most focussed and inspirational people I know. His down to earth approach, tremendous support and brilliant coaching from his mentoring group have been well worth the investment, and I can't thank him enough.

AND FINALLY . . .

One of the questions I'm often asked is 'Can ANYBODY be an entrepreneur like you Simon?'

The answer is a resounding YES. Even if you don't consider yourself to be a 'born' entrepreneur, have an 'instinctive' nose for business or a 'naturally' opportunistic personality, after coaching thousands of students over the years I am convinced that ANYBODY can learn to make money on the Internet. The key is you have to WANT to do it, and if you are sufficiently motivated and prepared to put in the work and commitment you can learn all the skills necessary to succeed. It's all about believing in YOU.

Looking back, I have to admit that as a child I did show some entrepreneurial traits. For instance, when I went on a school trip to France at the age of 11 my mum gave me the equivalent of £5 spending money. Just before we boarded the coach to return to the UK I realised I hadn't bought Mum a present, so I ran in a shop to see what I could buy. I picked up a baguette and thought Mum would be delighted with that, and then I realised that loads of the other kids hadn't bought their mum a present either, so I bought a job lot with all the money I had left. When I got back on the coach I sold the baguettes to the other kids at 5x the cost price, and came home with more money than I'd left with!

At 12 I started a leaflet delivery service. This began when a neighbour asked my mum if my older brother, who was 16, if he wanted a job delivering leaflets for his portrait artist business around the neighbourhood. My brother wasn't interested so I put my hand up, glad of the chance to earn a few pounds. To carry the leaflets I customised an old sports bag by Sellotaping a hand-written label on the side saying 'Delivery Service'. I thought if I look professional like this I could get more business from other locals, but despite spending a fortune on my own branded delivery sack I never did get any more clients! If you want a laugh take a look at a photo of my bag in the picture section.

Don't be put off if YOU don't consider yourself to have an obvious flair for making money, or if you have tried and failed in the past, or feel you have missed the boat and left it too late in life. I didn't recognise MY entrepreneurial skills until I was well into my 30s. It is NEVER too late, as some of my students have proved, launching successful businesses in their 70s and even 80s.

Also, there are MANY types of successful entrepreneurs and you just need to find out which of your personality traits can be exploited to help you grow a successful business.

Several years ago, out of interest, I analysed my personality using a well-known 'Wealth Dynamics' test created by a guy called Roger Hamilton. It's a popular profiling tool for entrepreneurs, resulting from years of studying successful wealth creators combined with Chinese philosophy. I was a bit sceptical I suppose, but the idea is that once you know your 'wealth profile' you can use that information to help you progress in business, so I gave it a go.

My test showed I am an 'idea generator' and a 'system maker' – or a 'creator' and a 'mechanic' to use the jargon as it was described to me at the time. This fitted with my history: I'd had a string of ideas, and I'd created systems to 'rinse and repeat' to capitalise on my ideas and replicate my success. Along the way I constantly refined my systems while never stopping to look for new ideas. In short, without planning to, I had played to my personality strengths, and this is what YOU can do too.

Very importantly, it doesn't matter if you aren't an 'ideas' person or you don't consider yourself to have the sort of brain that can clearly see how to 'systemise' a winning formula. Your strengths may lie in other areas. Perhaps you are blessed with bags of charisma that make you a great leader or motivator, or you may be a natural bargain-hunter, a talented deal-maker or a fantastic networker who works well in a team or in a joint venture.

Be honest with yourself and write a list of your 10 strongest personality traits – or you could even pay for a *Wealth Dynamics* test like I did (it currently costs $97 – see *wealthdynamics.com*).

Then consider how you can play to YOUR strengths as you develop your business. Conversely, if there is a crucial part of your business that you really do not feel suited to, don't be put off. Consider recruiting a friend to help you out in the early stages, or think about outsourcing. A successful business person has to overcome hurdles and find solutions, and bringing in other personalities to make things work may be the smartest move you make.

As my case study students show throughout this book, people of all ages and from all walks of life can learn to make their fortune online if they set their mind to it and put in the work. Very few of my students – if any – thought they were born to make 6 or 7-figure sums, or to be natural Interpreneurs. They simply believed in their business idea, wanted to make a success of it and put in the time and effort to learn HOW.

At the end of the photo section you'll see a picture of me on stage at the Brighton Centre in October 2016, receiving a standing ovation for my business speech. It's a fitting closure to this book as that was the very same stage I'd seen Coldplay perform on in 2002, which started my whole journey to becoming an Interpreneur. Who would have thought the idea I had when I was driving home from that gig, to start a Coldplay tribute band, would have set me on the road to building my million pound businesses, performing at the O2 arena, speaking alongside Sirs, Dames, Lords and former presidents, holidaying on Necker Island, buying a brand new Ferrari and teaching around the world? And who would have dreamed that when I watched The Darling Buds of May with Grandma on a Sunday evening in 1991-1993 that one day I'd own that little piece of paradise? What's more, who would have believed that those decisions would not only change my own life beyond all recognition, but enable me to change 100s of other peoples' fortunes for the better too?

So maybe if you dare to dream, your dreams might just come true, make it happen and take some action.

Believe in yourself, because YOU could be the next case study I'm writing about, and you could be the next Interpreneur millionaire. It's up to you to make the first move, so visit *Interpreneur.com*/**resources** TODAY. There you can register for extra resources, updates and get a free online marketing course to set you on your way.

Good luck!